D1322916

A scientist by background, Moira Curry ⟨illegible⟩ ⟨illegible⟩ ⟨illegible⟩ ⟨illegible⟩ ⟨illegible⟩ ⟨illegible⟩ ⟨illegible⟩cation for over 25 years, with responsibility for Science, RE and Collective Worship in the schools where she taught.

Moira has now left paid teaching to devote more time to children's work, and to develop her role with a small UK charity that works alongside an economically deprived village community in Uganda. Part of her church worship team, she is also a trained listener and tutor for Acorn Christian Healing Trust. Married to Richard, with three grown-up children, Moira enjoys singing, creative textile work, producing handmade books, walking and swimming.

Gill Morgan grew up in Chester and trained as a primary school teacher, specialising in music. Married to Gareth, she taught for three years before leaving to concentrate on bringing up their four children, now grown up. After several years running music workshops for preschool children, Gill returned to teaching, spending ten years teaching RE, Music and Arts in a village school.

Since 2000 Gill and Gareth have been involved with a development programme for a village in Eastern Uganda, the growth of which contributed to her giving up teaching in 2003. Gill and Moira import and sell crafts from Uganda to support the projects, as well as giving promotional presentations. Gill and Gareth are local leaders for The Marriage Course. Gill's interests include cooking for family and friends, gardening, walking, photography and creative textile work. Her chocolate brownie is legendary.

Moira and Gill have been involved in a range of children's activities in their church and community, including lunch, after-school and holiday clubs, and have been part of the children's team at Spring Harvest. They are also Scripture Union affiliates and have trialled new material for the organisation. The development of this work led them into heading up the Christmas Journey and Easter Journey teams at Main St Community Church in Frodsham, Cheshire.

Text copyright © Moira Curry and Gill Morgan 2009
The authors assert the moral right
to be identified as the authors of this work

Published by
The Bible Reading Fellowship
15 The Chambers, Vineyard
Abingdon OX14 3FE
United Kingdom
Tel: +44 (0)1865 319700
Email: enquiries@brf.org.uk
Website: www.brf.org.uk

ISBN 978 1 84101 622 1

First published 2009
10 9 8 7 6 5 4 3 2 1 0

Acknowledgments
Unless otherwise stated, scripture quotations are taken from the Contemporary English Version
of the Bible published by HarperCollins Publishers, copyright © 1991, 1992, 1995 American
Bible Society.

A catalogue record for this book is available from the British Library

Printed in Singapore by Craft Print International Ltd

The Easter Journey

An imaginative presentation
for churches to use with primary schools

Moira Curry and Gill Morgan

Foreword by Gail Fullbrook,
Head Teacher, Frodsham C of E Primary School

✳

To our (now grown up) children who always willingly—
if sometimes unwittingly—joined in our earlier   ✳
ventures, which led to this journey. Thank you for still
believing in us.

Acknowledgments

Thanks go to Helen Franklin, whose encouragement and
belief in us has sent us on many exciting 'journeys'
over the years, including this one.

Thank you, too, to Martin Ansdell-Smith for so generously
sharing his expertise in setting up and maintaining the
Easter Journey website.

To all those who have given support, skills and advice in the
putting together of the book: we are truly grateful.

Thank you to Martyn Payne for his invaluable
help and inspiration.

Finally, and most importantly, heartfelt thanks go to the
entire *Easter Journey* team, each one of you making your
own very special contribution, and without whom
none of this could have happened.

Comments on The Easter Journey experience

I thought the whole presentation was excellent. The children were so well behaved and engaged with everything beautifully. The set and environment were very well done and gave me food for thought for work in my own situation.

SCRIPTURE UNION WORKER

A group of normally noisy, active children sit enthralled by the challenge of the Easter story. Pupils and teachers are visibly moved by the experiences of Mary and Peter. These are just two pictures of the impact of The Easter Journey *in Frodsham. After the groups have made their way through the various scenes of the story, we sit with them to ask which part they like best or want to talk about. Helpers go through the journey several times in the week but each time is fresh as the children share their reactions. If you are looking for a relevant way to share the oldest and greatest story ever told,* The Easter Journey *is a highly effective means which will stay in children's, teachers' and helpers' memories for a long time.*

PASTOR, MAIN STREET COMMUNITY CHURCH

Thank you for such a moving and powerful morning. It was a wonderful way to begin our Holy Week. The children were totally absorbed by the whole event and their feedback was very deep and thoughtful.

HEAD TEACHER

My favourite part was:
- *When we were making pictures out of stones and the story of the vineyard.*
- *All of it, but especially the last supper, because you felt you were really there.*

- *Hiding behind bushes because we knew the Romans were coming to get Jesus. I felt quite frightened.*
- *The people at the church, because they were so friendly, and I enjoyed selling things in the temple.*
- *When Peter and Mary spoke, because it was as if I knew how Peter felt.*
- *When we waved palm leaves, as it really made me feel one of the crowd.*
- *The last supper, because it felt as if I was a friend of Jesus.*

YEAR 5 CHILDREN

Contents

Foreword..11

Introduction 12

Part One: Preparing for the event

Framework for the presentation 22

The church community 25

The local primary schools..38

Checklists 42

Sample invitation..44

Sample prayer card 45

Sample risk assessment form...46

Creating the journey..48

Part Two: The Easter Journey

Introductory warm-up...54

Scene 1: Palm Sunday 58

Scene 2: In the temple...62

Scene 3: The stone that the builders rejected 65

Scene 4: The last supper 72

Scene 5: The garden of Gethsemane...77

Scene 6: The crucifixion...81

Scene 7: The day in between...90

Scene 8: The resurrection garden 93

Discussion and conclusion 98

Part Three: After The Easter Journey

Follow-up activities.. 104

Suggested plan of rooms... 121

Resources... 122

*

Foreword

Opening up the Easter story to children is not easy. It's a story of great contrasts: joy and sadness, wonder and disbelief, horror and excitement. And yet it's a story so central to the Christian faith that no matter what complexities it throws up, it needs to be told. As adults we come face to face with all that we know of God and of Jesus but struggle to explain. The challenge is to retell the story for children (and indeed for adults) in such a way that none of the mystery is lost.

In *The Easter Journey*, we're given a pattern, a way in, that will fascinate and encourage children to take steps in understanding.

The children of Frodsham have had the wonderful opportunity to travel this journey already. They have come to the journey from many faith backgrounds (and some from none), yet all have learned; all have gained something. For some children, the experience raises questions, gives a deeper insight and helps them to make sense of the world in which they live.

The Easter Journey, for me, is one of those lovely examples of God at work in his world. Through people like Moira Curry and Gill Morgan and the adults who join the 'production team', and through all who come to take part, seeds are sown of a story that has been changing people's lives for generations and, by God's grace, will continue to do so.

The practical footprints of the journey are laid out within these pages, so read, enjoy, share and, importantly, have a go.

Gail Fullbrook, Head Teacher, Frodsham C of E Primary School

✳

Introduction

Although Easter is the most important festival of the year for the Christian Church, it can be a confusing and difficult series of events to share with children. In many cases, commercialism has reduced the story to hot cross buns, chocolate eggs and fluffy bunnies—all of which make the reality of the historical events hard to relate to the present day. Death is a subject that is rarely discussed in the home and school nowadays. Although many children have experience of 'virtual' violent death on computer and TV screens, the topic is often thought to be best avoided.

The miraculous events of the first Easter are profound and amazing to Christians who themselves struggle to understand the mystery of Christ's victory over death and his work of forgiveness on the cross. Over the centuries, artists, authors, musicians and actors have tried to portray elements of the Holy Week story in paintings, choral works, plays, films and musical theatre. The story is considered so central to the Christian faith that all the Gospel writers devote proportionately more of their writing to the last few days of Jesus' life than to the years of his earlier ministry. The apostle Peter tells the dramatic story over and over again in Acts. If the resurrection had not happened, it is doubtful whether Christianity would have survived even the first century. Because it did, there is a tremendous story to tell and a hope that has enabled Christians to keep sharing their faith in the face of unimaginable difficulties and circumstances. The events of Holy Week have given rise to significant church traditions, celebration and sacrament, all of which make this festival a very important part of the school curriculum as well as the life of the local church.

The Easter journey in this book is not original and is little different from many other excellent resources available, which portray the same story. The presentation set out here is offered to schools and the local community as an experience so that those taking part in the story may enter into the wonder and mystery of the events. *The Easter Journey* travels with Jesus during the last few days of his life and leaves the participants to think about God's rescue plan for the world. The hope is that, having entered into this experience, both children and adults will understand the significance of the Easter story and the pivotal part that it plays in the whole Christian journey today.

This book is designed as a toolkit to enable churches to run their own presentation and is supported by the *Easter Journey* website, www.easterjourney.org.uk, where additional information can be accessed. The website provides photographs, plans and downloads for use in the presentation.

The book is divided into three sections. The first part provides the background and practical planning needed before the experience. There are hints about team training, enthusing the church family, publicity and links with schools. The second part gives a practical outline of the components of the event. There are lists of props, scenery and characters, together with scripts and suggestions for lighting and audio-visuals. The third section develops ideas for follow-up activities once schools have visited the presentation, to help to keep the experience alive and to promote discussion. There are ideas for all-age worship, assemblies and class lessons as well as further resources to complement the visit.

The outline

When visiting *The Easter Journey*, children and adults are led around key elements of some of the events of Holy Week in a thought-provoking way by leaders trained to help the participants respond at their own level of understanding. *The Easter Journey* is multi-sensory, lasts about an hour and can be adapted for different buildings and spaces. Essentially there are six storytelling areas, which relate to different parts of the Easter story. Each space develops part of the story. The group is led on a journey beginning with a warm-up, leading to a role-play about Palm Sunday and the clearing of the temple. The group then hears the story of the tenants in the vineyard. They move to a re-enactment of the last supper, creep out to hide behind bushes in the garden of Gethsemane, see an audiovisual portrayal of the crucifixion and hear powerful testimony from two of the characters who witnessed the death of Jesus. From here they enter the low point of the darkness of the next day before coming out into the brilliant light of the garden tomb and resurrection, where they are told the amazing news of Jesus' resurrection. Finally, they move back to the first area for a group discussion and are asked to reflect on the experience and think about the ongoing story today.

The presentation is designed primarily for Year 5 children so that schools may be invited annually. Year 5 was chosen to be the focus because of the nature of the events of Holy Week. At this age, children are developing thinking skills and opinions and are trying to make sense of the bigger questions of life. They are able to think in a more abstract way, relating stories to their own experience, and to link events in a historical timeline. The expectation is that the experience will build on the work already done on *The Christmas Journey*, which children may have experienced in Year 2. *The Christmas Journey* is a separate but similar event designed for younger children (see pages 122 and 123 for details of the website and book).

Although *The Easter Journey* is designed primarily for children, in its original setting in the Cheshire town of Frodsham it is open to the general public for an evening session, enabling children to return with families and other adults to visit. Linking this opening with invitations to special all-age Easter services and events can provide a useful tool for reaching out into the community.

Much of the content of the book is based on the experience of running *The Easter Journey* in a small church in Frodsham. Anyone reading the book and wanting to run the event themselves will no doubt approach the project from different situations and with different opportunities. However, it may be useful and encouraging to hear how the story in Frodsham began and how God led us on a faith journey, both as individuals and as a team, from small beginnings.

The journey begins

We had been running *The Christmas Journey* for a few years when the inevitable question was raised on several occasions, 'When are you going to put on an Easter journey?' We had felt that we should look into presenting something along similar lines for older children, so it didn't take much encouragement for us to look into the possibilities.

Strangely enough, it had been through seeing a presentation of an Easter journey at a church in Crewe that we had originally been inspired to put together our own Christmas journey. Although we as a church are not part of a recognised denomination, we have links in our area with many different churches. Through our local Anglican diocese's regular bulletin of events that could interest others, we had read of an Easter journey that was to take place in Crewe a few weeks later. We had arranged to go and have a look and were amazed to discover a happy atmosphere of primary school children alongside keen and willing volunteers portraying the story of that first Easter in a variety of different ways, including drama, language and singing.

We had decided that we would start by exploring a Christmas journey. We felt that Christmas was more readily recognised by schools as something they might be interested in. The previous year, our town had held a Christmas festival. This was a civic-run event involving the whole town in a variety of activities, none of which, though fun to be part of, had any direct link with the events of the first Christmas. We realised that a Christmas journey could be the churches' way of offering something to the festival. You can read how our Christmas journey came together in our book, *The Christmas Journey* (see page 123 for details).

Exploring the idea

We knew that an Easter journey would be more appropriate for older children than the Year 2 children who come along to our Christmas journey presentations each year. The events of the first Easter require a more mature mind. We felt it was important to present the journey in such a way that the children would leave feeling that they had been part of the experience. It wasn't enough to tell them facts; rather, we wanted to involve them in the emotions of the events. We knew that Year 6 children would, by this stage, in their final year at primary school, have a lot of other activities and distractions going on, so we settled on Year 5 as our target group.

The first steps

We made a list of the events that we thought important for the children to experience and decided that we had to involve participatory drama, as well as storytelling. We were aware that portraying the crucifixion would present difficulties from the point of view of how much detail to go into, and wondered whether technology could provide a solution.

The way we used the space would need to be different from *The Christmas Journey*, for which we used six very similar-sized rooms. Apart from anything else, the children would all be going round the journey together in one big group, and 30 or so Year 5 children take up a lot more room than 15 Year 2s.

The team

Having a ready-made team who had all been used to helping us on *The Christmas Journey*, it was time to find out how many would be willing to give up more time for *The Easter Journey*. Once again, many of the helpers would be from other churches in the town, since we have a strong history of working together with other churches. We knew that the help needed for *The Easter Journey* would be less role-specific but still it was important for everyone to feel valued.

God confirms the plans

During the development of the initial plans for our Christmas journey, a Bible verse was repeatedly coming to the fore. In Matthew 13, Jesus tells the parable of the farmer, in which some of his seed falls along the road and is eaten by birds. Other seed falls on thin, rocky ground and quickly wilts because the soil isn't very deep. More seeds fall where thorn bushes grow up and choke the plants. But a few seeds fall on good ground where the plants produce 30, 60 or 100 times as much as was scattered. As we reflected on this and read on, we felt that God was saying, 'This next bit applies to you and what I am asking you to do with *The Christmas Journey*.' Matthew 13:35 says, 'I will use stories to speak my message and to explain things that have been hidden since the creation of the world.' This seemed to be saying that here was an ideal opportunity to spread God's word (the seed) through the retelling of the great story of his plan for humankind. We subsequently used this verse on the *Christmas Journey* prayer cards and decided to use Psalm 78:3–4 on the *Easter Journey* prayer cards: 'These are things we learnt from our ancestors, and we will tell them to the next generation. We won't keep secret the glorious deeds and the mighty miracles of the Lord.' (See page 37 for further information about the *Easter Journey* prayer card, and page 45 for a sample).

Moving on

Feeling that we had reached the point of no return and that we just had to get on and plan *The Easter Journey*, we arranged to meet a friend who is very experienced in working with children in schools and churches. We wanted to talk over the possibilities and ideas we already had, and to see if he had any further suggestions that would inspire us.

This involved a train journey to a mutually convenient halfway point, where we spent the entire day in the first café we came across, initially with coffee, progressing to lunch and finishing with tea and cake before catching our respective trains back home. We found the time beneficial and later discovered that the café was a Christian centre, supported by the churches of the town, which offered prayer as part of its ministry. We certainly felt God's guidance during our meeting, so in some ways our discovery was hardly surprising!

Among other things, we particularly wanted to explore the possibility of finding a small 'take-home' gift for the children—something to remind them of their Easter journey—just as we had with *The Christmas Journey*. Despite visiting local Christian bookshops, asking other contacts and trawling websites, we were still having trouble addressing this issue. That day, during our marathon visit to the café, between the three of us we devised an idea that developed into a good-quality booklet (visit www.easterjourney.org. uk for details).

The final touches

After returning from our three-way meeting, our Easter journey really began to take shape. We had a training day to which we invited everyone who was interested in being on the team. There was an opportunity for the team, in smaller groups, to work on ideas for the scripts for Mary's and Peter's speeches in the crucifixion scene.

There was still just one more vital element. Without schools to attend, all our work would be in vain. We were fortunate to have an established relationship with the local primary schools, which had improved even further since we had been running *The Christmas Journey*. If you have not yet established a relationship with your local primary schools, see page 38 for some suggestions on how to do so. Schools nowadays are expected to be part of a cluster, working with other schools in many areas, and head teachers will readily recommend something good to other heads. As soon as schools heard about *The Easter Journey*, they quickly signed up to come.

There were many other affirming moments from God in the devising of our Easter journey, but the support of the churches, the team, the faces of the children and the response of the adult visitors made this a very special event in the life of our church and community. Our tentative small steps have been richly blessed.

Part One

Preparing for the event

*

Framework for the presentation

The Easter Journey is designed so that the whole experience lasts for an hour, suitable for groups of up to 30 children.

When they first arrive, visitors are asked to sit down in a suitable area and are welcomed to *The Easter Journey*. Once they are seated, the storyteller explains to the group that they are going on a journey to learn about and experience the last days of Jesus' life. He or she begins with a warm-up exercise, which leads into the first role-play about Palm Sunday. Each scene is described in detail in Part Two of the book (see pages 54–101). However, the basic structure for the journey is as follows:

Warm-up and Palm Sunday	10 minutes
In the temple	5 minutes
The stone that the builders rejected	5 minutes
The last supper	5 minutes
The garden of Gethsemane	5 minutes
The crucifixion	4 minutes
Mary's and Peter's story	7 minutes
The day in between	2 minutes
The resurrection garden	6 minutes
Group discussion	9 minutes

Although these timings look very precise, they are just a guide and you need to allow for a little flexibility. Much will depend on the size and responsiveness of the group. However, it is important for leaders to be aware of time in order to make sure that all elements of the story are experienced fully before the next school arrives. It may be tempting to cut down time for discussion but this would leave out valuable time in the journey for children to reflect upon and respond to the things they have seen and heard.

Sample timetable for one school visit

Each scene should be carefully planned so that timings can be followed as closely as possible. Some activities take longer than others but it is essential that the whole journey does not last longer than the hour allotted.

Time	Activity
9.30am	Warm-up and Palm Sunday
9.40am	In the temple
9.45am	The stone that the builders rejected
9.50am	The last supper
9.55am	The garden of Gethsemane
10.00am	The crucifixion
10.04am	Mary's and Peter's story
10.11am	The day in between
10.13am	The resurrection garden
10.19am	Group discussion
10.28am	Conclusion

Suggested daily timetable for several school visits

The above timing will mean that you will be able to allow for a maximum of four school sessions per day. With the maximum number of visiting schools, the morning sessions last from 9.30am until 10.30am, and 10.45am until 11.45am. This allows for a short changeover slot. Afternoon sessions begin at 12.45pm until 1.45pm, then 1.45pm until 2.45pm, thus allowing pupils to return to school for home time. The schools that attend the 12.45pm slot will often arrange for the pupils attending to have an early lunch that day. It is also worth considering the proximity of the final schools of the day, perhaps giving a warning in case the event overruns by a few minutes.

9.00 am	Team meet for prayer and preparation
9.30–10.30 am	School 1
10.45–11.45am	School 2
12.45–1.45 pm	School 3
1.45–2.45 pm	School 4

If several schools are visiting in one day, there are several important points to consider to make sure the day runs smoothly.

- Try to use a one-way system of entrances and exits if your building allows for this, so that, if one school arrives as another is leaving, there is no confusion.
- A holding area is useful so that, should a school arrive early, there will be time for introductions and to watch part of a suitable video without disturbing the previous school.
- The children need a place to remove and store their coats.

*

The church community

Once you have decided to put on *The Easter Journey* yourself, there are several considerations to take into account. For example, if the event is to take place just before Easter, detailed planning should begin early in the New Year—although it would be wise to inform your church council or Churches Together team of your thoughts before this, so that prayer and the logistics of dates can be factored into the church calendar. The dates for Easter vary year by year and careful note should be taken of the dates of school holidays in your area. The nearer to Holy Week the event is planned, the more relevant it is to the school curriculum.

As Christians, we are inviting schools to take part in an event that shows the church community working together to produce an experience that is both exciting and of a high standard. Schools nowadays have come to expect sophisticated high-tech events and our task is to present the Easter story in an attractive professional way without detracting from the biblical narrative. This can be a good opportunity to show your local community that the church is relevant and up to date.

Creating a team

The event will need a team of enthusiastic people who are able to work together to provide an exciting and thought-provoking experience for the visitors. If your church is small, you could invite other churches to work together to expand the team. Churches Together or a similar local group would provide a good platform from which to share the vision and recruit helpers. It may be useful to ask for time in Sunday services at other churches to explain the idea and encourage helpers. Notice sheets, church magazines and personal invitations can be effective. It is important that the church community provides an experience for schools that is both enjoyable and professional. Working together with other Christians as part of the team can be a real blessing to those involved as well as a valuable witness to visitors.

So what kind of team is needed to put on *The Easter Journey*? The lists below suggest the maximum number of people needed, both before and during the event. However, if people are in short supply, many of these roles can be doubled up, as some of them are required only for short periods of time. Assigning helpers to a specific job or jobs helps the team to have clarity of purpose and a feeling of value and responsibility. Once a list of specific tasks is drawn up, you will be amazed at the skills that people feel that they can offer. The church family can develop ownership of the event and use many skills and gifts in preparation.

Helpers needed in preparation for the event

- Leaders/coordinator(s): This can be one person or a small team, but it is essential that those involved in *The Easter Journey* have someone to oversee the whole event, to take responsibility for the smooth running of the event and to delegate and troubleshoot where necessary. As the Frodsham journey was the inspiration and vision of two people, a shared leadership has worked well.
- Layout and logistical planning: The layout is dependent on the premises and the creative use of facilities available. A small team can discuss ideas and plan the sequence and smooth transition between rooms.
- Costumes and props providers: A list of costumes and props required for the scenes can be circulated in the church. This can bring surprising results as, for example, people who are reluctant to work with children or take leading roles find that they can often offer sewing skills or supply items to be used for props.
- Scenery makers: However simple or complicated the scenery is to be, a certain amount of preparation and design is needed before the event. On pages 54–101, the scenes are described

in detail, so it should be possible for a small group to prepare scenery in advance of set-up.

- **Refreshment team leader:** Ideally, you need to find a volunteer who can take overall responsibility for providing refreshments for the visiting staff and the team. There may be helpers who do not wish to work directly with the children but who would be happy to fill this role.
- **Administration:** Invitations need to be sent out to schools, follow-up needs to be arranged, and transport needs to be booked if the church is providing it. A sample invitation is given on pages 44–45. Prayer cards need to be produced (see page 45) and T-shirts ordered if required.
- **Publicity officers:** If the general public is to be invited, adverts and publicity will need to be placed in local schools and churches.

Helpers needed during the event

- **Leaders/organisers:** As mentioned before, the overall leadership can be shared. It is better for the leader or leaders not to have a prime role in the actual event. This releases them to be available if there are any problems with schools, buses, props and other issues. It also means that they are able to chat to teachers and monitor timings to ensure the smooth running of *The Easter Journey*. The leaders will know most about all aspects of the journey, so they will be the best troubleshooters.
- **Group leaders:** The children will be split into groups of four to six. Each group requires a leader to escort the children through the journey and encourage them to participate fully in the experience. The group leaders will lead their group from scene to scene, linking the scenes together, and will guide the discussion session at the end. It is best if they have experience of working with children, are able to speak confidently and are not easily flustered if things don't always go according to plan.
- **Group leaders' assistants:** If enough helpers with leading skills are available, an assistant leader with each group can be helpful,

although it is acceptable to have just one leader with Year 5 children. The groups will all travel round the journey together and it is important that everyone, both adults and children, are encouraged to participate in the experience.

- **Storyteller:** The storyteller begins the experience for the children by facilitating the warm-up. He or she then leads them into the Palm Sunday scene and helps them to enact the drama of the clearing of the temple. After this, the storyteller tells the story of the stone that the builders rejected. He or she meets the groups again in the resurrection garden and explains the events of the first Easter day. Finally, after the discussion, the storyteller shares the booklet with the children. Although it is not absolutely necessary to use the same person for all these scenes, there is better continuity if the same storyteller begins and ends the journey.

- **Actors:** Three actors are needed for the parts of Jesus, Peter and Mary, the mother of Jesus. The actor playing the part of Jesus is needed in the last supper scene. Mary and Peter speak movingly about their feelings after witnessing the crucifixion.

- **Refreshment team:** Providing refreshments for accompanying adults is an important part of the final session. As the children come to the end of the experience and sit in discussion groups, teachers can be offered a comfortable place to sit in sight of the children, but in a separate area of the room, with good-quality resources to browse. (See page 123 for suggested resources for teachers.) Helpers can offer tea and coffee with hot cross buns or Easter biscuits. This is a valuable opportunity for building good relationships with the school staff. Team members will also appreciate refreshments when they have a break between their tasks.

- **Technical support:** There are some technological requirements for *The Easter Journey*, such as the switching on of lights, DVDs and CDs at appropriate times. Team members who have other roles can provide this support where necessary if help is limited.

For example, the actor playing Jesus leaves the last supper scene before the children and therefore can switch on the sound effects for the garden of Gethsemane.

- **Gatekeepers, meeters and greeters:** It is important that someone is responsible for making sure no child leaves the building during school visits. If the next school arrives before the previous one has left, someone needs to be available to explain what to do and make the new school feel welcome. Coats need to be in place for children who are leaving and timings coordinated. It is important to allocate at least two people to these tasks.

Team training

In order to encourage a friendly and welcoming attitude to the visitors, the *Easter Journey* team may find the following guidelines helpful. It is useful, when building a team, to incorporate the issues highlighted below into a training session for helpers. Team members will have the opportunity to ask questions about issues that concern them and a code of conduct can be agreed. It is important that the team recognises the leadership structure and knows whom to approach with suggestions or problems. Leaders should be able to give account of their actions and know how to affirm their team. The training session should include an overview of the event, discussion of scenes in detail and ideas for talking to children. It is useful for helpers to have an idea of the 'big picture' to understand where their part fits into the whole and that there may be sound reasons for doing something in a particular way.

It is important for the team to be aware of child protection issues, although there should be no need for helpers to be alone with a child because groups will be accompanied by school staff. However, it is highly desirable that each helper holds a CRB enhanced certificate. The current UK Government policy is clearly explained by the Churches Child Protection Advisory Service (CCPAS). CCPAS provide invaluable advice and practical help to churches about child protection issues. For more information, visit www.ccpas.co.uk.

Good practice guidelines must be understood and followed by team members. Appropriate behaviour when helping children should be discussed in team training. For example, care must be taken when working closely alongside the children, not to use inappropriate touch. Adults who are not used to working with children in a professional capacity sometimes cannot see the harm in putting an arm around a child or accompanying a child alone to the toilet. As a church, however, we need to show teachers and parents that we not only understand and uphold child protection laws but support the reasoning behind them.

It is also important that helpers are aware that this is not an opportunity to attempt to convert children to Christianity. The story is being offered to the children and adults to help them to reflect upon the real meaning of Easter and the reason why Jesus died and came back to life. The prayer is that seeds are sown, which will take root, but it is still part of an educational experience for the children and teachers. The locally agreed syllabus requires that children know the facts about the story of the first Easter and are able to respond to it. They are encouraged to wonder about the world and Jesus' life and death, but not to make a decision about their personal faith. Many children will be from homes where the Easter story is not familiar, and some may be of other faiths. Sensitivity is vital in order to develop and maintain trust between the Christian community and the schools.

Encourage the team to focus on what is happening all the time. Even if they don't have a major role in an activity, such as when the children are taking part in role-play or listening to a story, explain to them that it is important to be joining in with the children rather than chatting or getting on with other preparation. If adult helpers are seen to be involved at all times with the children, it encourages the accompanying staff to participate in the journey.

Training day outline

Time	Activity
10.00am	Welcome, introductions and opportunity for prayer and worship
10.30am	Outline of the journey: the big picture
11.15am	Coffee
11.30am	Team-building task, such as working on a logo together or writing scripts for Mary and Peter (sample scripts are available on pages 85–89).
12.30pm	Lunch
1.30pm	Guidelines and questions about working with children. Discussion of child protection issues and the importance of referring any problem to the leader(s). Guidelines about sensitivity when working with children and the importance of not proselytising.
2.15pm	Tea
2.30pm	Work through the Palm Sunday scene, or the story of the stone that the builders rejected, using a storyteller. Discuss the questions in the final activity. Encourage the team to think of open-ended questions to use with the children and consider the space needed for children to participate in discussion.
3.30–4.00pm	Time of personal reflection and prayer for the event

Budget

It is difficult to be accurate about the amount of money required to put on *The Easter Journey*. If your church has an outreach budget, it is worth remembering that this event will bring in a significant number of people who will all hear the story of Jesus. Costs will vary depending on the scale of the project and the materials used, but an important consideration is that most costs will be 'one off', so, if you are planning the event to take place annually, the overall cost will drop significantly in subsequent years. Setting up the Frodsham *Easter Journey* cost approximately £500 for the materials, including gazebos, fabrics, plants, corrugated card, paint and timber. As a result of the success of *The Christmas Journey*, we anticipated that schools would appreciate the Easter production as an annual event, so we ordered polo shirts for the team, professionally printed with the *Easter Journey* logo.

There are costs for materials, refreshments, publicity and take-home booklets. (We designed our own folding booklet and had it professionally printed. Details are available from the *Easter Journey* website: www.easterjourney.org.uk). Often, these costs are met by individual gifts, although it is important to take into account the money spent so that, if anyone else takes over the running of the event, they will understand the need to make the church aware of the budget. If money is a problem, it should not be a barrier to a successful *Easter Journey* presentation, as many things can be borrowed and adapted. A little creativity goes a long way!

Dates and times

A major consideration, when planning your event, is the number of days you are realistically able to commit to *The Easter Journey*. This will depend on the size of your team, availability of the premises, the number of schools you would like to invite and so on. *The Easter Journey* at Frodsham began with three days and subsequently progressed to four days as more schools heard about the presentation and wanted an invitation. A larger team could share the workload, enabling more sessions to be offered.

The Easter Journey is ideally presented as near to the end of the spring term as possible. Much depends on the timing of Easter, which changes from year to year. Staff can use the event to stimulate discussion and learning in the lead-up to Easter. If the church can offer coach transport to and from the event, this is very helpful for schools at a busy time of the year. It is worth asking local councils or businesses for help towards costs, or even to offer to hire a coach and split the cost between the participating schools. It will be cheaper and will make the experience more pleasurable for the staff. It also allows more control over the arrival and departure of children.

Organising the event just before Easter gives an ideal opportunity to invite staff, children and families to Easter events at the church and in the local Christian community.

The venue

The way in which *The Easter Journey* is created depends on the size and layout of your venue. The main presentation area should be divided into five or six separate storytelling rooms (described in detail in Part Two). It is useful if the first area is in a different part of the building from the main body of the journey experience, and a holding area is useful for groups arriving early. Toilets and emergency exits should be clearly labelled and children and adults need to know what fire procedures are in place.

The journey should flow as seamlessly as possible from one scene to another, so it is worth considering the creative use of your whole building. The first activities require a reasonable space to allow for controlled movement, but other scenes can be in smaller rooms and need to be ready for the children to take part as soon as they enter. Some areas can be used more than once. For example, the area used in Frodsham for the story of the stone that the builders rejected is quickly converted into a resurrection garden while the children are on the later parts of the journey. Some areas need to be darkened, others bright and welcoming. The children travel through the journey as one large group so there is no need to soundproof rooms.

School staff

An important part of the final session is to provide a comfortable waiting area for the school staff who accompany each group, so that they are able to have coffee and tea and look at resources suitable for RE and Citizenship. Teachers are normally responsible for children for the whole of an educational visit, so a short break, in a place where they can still see the children but are being looked after themselves, can be very welcome. This is a useful time for the team leaders or church minister to chat to the visiting staff, explaining *The Easter Journey* and perhaps offering help with assemblies linked to this or other Christian events if they feel able to.

Additional materials

It is worth thinking about adding other experiences to *The Easter Journey*, so that there is something else for the children to do if they have some spare time. In Frodsham, a display of crosses from around the world has provided an added attraction for the helpers to show the children. These are readily available from fair trade organisations such as Tearcraft, Traidcraft, Oxfam and so on, and a plea for the congregation to lend them can be very productive. Some crosses can be fragile and it is important that children are asked to respect this fact. It is useful to have a selection of children's Easter storybooks available. See pages 123–124 for a suggested range of resources; also, the local library can provide books if given enough notice.

Branding and logos

The idea of branding and using logos may be unfamiliar to some members of the church family, but it can make the event more cohesive and professional in nature. Children nowadays are used to sophisticated marketing, so choosing a logo and using it in all publications, information and even on helpers' T-shirts can help to create a sense of belonging and identity for both the team and the participants. If you decide to give children a book or pamphlet to take home, it is good to use an image linked to this.

Lifewords (www.sgmlifewords.com) and other publishers produce appropriate literature for Easter and they will often provide free downloads of the images for PowerPoint presentations and publicity. There may be someone in the church family who is experienced in this field and can create the logo and advise on its use. Downloads of clip-art from the Internet could be another avenue to explore. T-shirts can be branded using iron-on computer-generated images. If the budget is small, badges are easy to produce. You could even use sticky labels on a coloured shirt, with the colour agreed between the team beforehand. T-shirts can later be printed professionally if the presentation becomes an annual event. The *Easter Journey* website (www.easterjourney.org.uk) provides downloads and links to useful resources for branding.

Dealing with the public

Although *The Easter Journey* is primarily designed for use with school children, it is possible to open the event to the public. Often, children will be anxious to have the opportunity to bring parents and siblings back to take part in the journey themselves. Extending the event to encompass weekend or evening opening will provide the public with an opportunity to take part in the experience. It may be worth introducing a ticketing system for journey times because of the limit on numbers. Remember, too, that children taking part in *The Easter Journey* during the open sessions need to be accompanied by a responsible adult at all times. Journey guides will need to adapt their presentation of the scenes in order to allow for a wider age range. Refreshments can be served and a friendly atmosphere created— again useful as outreach into the community. It is important that helpers are aware of numbers entering and exiting the building to ensure a smooth flow of visitors.

Health and safety

Schools may need to see a copy of the risk assessment for the event. A sample copy is available on pages 46–47. Health and safety issues, such as allergies, should always be considered (for example, when asking children to taste matzo bread, or with regard to the effect of flashing lights, if used, and the safety of electrical equipment in proximity to the visitors). Numbers should be monitored so that there are not too many visitors in each storytelling room. The management of children and adults leaving the building is just as important as the welcome. A leader should make sure that each group has all the coats and booklets they are expecting so that the whole experience is pleasant from beginning to end.

As the children relate to their leader, the assigned guide should be aware that it is part of their responsibility to ensure continuity.

Children with special needs can benefit greatly from the multi-sensory approach to the story and it can be an amazing and rewarding experience to lead such a group round *The Easter Journey*. Their responses may be very individual depending on their level of understanding, but teachers greatly value the event for their children. Helpers need to be sensitive to such groups, and guides may need to adapt to the needs of pupils. In this situation, small groups of children work best as special schools usually bring plenty of helpers trained in looking after the pupils. Their responses can be profound, although it may be advisable to be more flexible with timing and to omit the discussion time. *The Easter Journey* is designed for Year 5 children in mainstream schools, but it would be advisable to discuss with individual special schools when deciding who to invite to the journey. For example, Key Stage 3 children may appreciate the experience more than younger children.

Encouragement and prayer

In order for each team member to be affirmed and able to reflect upon the reason for the event, it is helpful to begin each day of *The Easter Journey* with a short time of prayer before getting on with practical tasks. Also, completing the event with a time of prayer and worship can be very worthwhile. Ideally, of course, *The Easter Journey* should be surrounded in prayer from the earliest preparation through to the event and afterwards. As well as church prayer groups, there may be local groups who pray specifically for schools, and it is good to keep them informed of needs and progress. Encouraging the church family to pray for specific needs can help to create ownership and a feeling of being part of the excitement of the event. Regular updates, either by email or in person, are valuable. Prayer cards that use the branding and perhaps a significant Bible verse are useful to hand out at local churches and Christian events. These are likely to be in the public domain so care should be taken about personal details and wording. The sample shown on page 45 is also available on the website, www.easterjourney.org.uk.

*

The local primary schools

Contacting schools

Many churches already have a good relationship with their local primary schools. Building such links is vital, not just in order to bring children into the church but also to offer genuine assistance to hard-pressed staff. Members of your congregation may already serve as school governors or help with reading, sport or assemblies where appropriate. Creating such opportunities can lead to a mutual respect and trust between the church and school. Groups set up to pray for the school can offer confidential prayer, and groups from churches are often involved in running after-school or lunchtime clubs.

It is important to be sensitive to the educational needs and aims of the school. It would be sad if years of prayer and careful nurturing of relationships were spoiled by an overenthusiastic, confessional approach. If a relationship of trust is built up, then an invitation to *The Easter Journey* will probably be well received and appreciated. Local schools often operate a cluster system, so that having a good relationship with one school may lead to recommendations to others. It is worth taking time to research this, as a friendly head teacher is a great asset in publicising your event.

Invitations should be sent out before the spring half-term. Schools plan their curriculum well in advance and often organise special events near the end of this term, so plenty of notice is advisable. It is best to allocate a particular slot to each school rather than giving them a choice. The school will soon ask to swap if their session is at an inconvenient time. If coach transport is offered, make pick-up and return times clear to the school, as this allows more control over the arrival and departure of children. It is useful to ask the coach company for a driver's mobile number just in case there are any hitches on the day.

Guidelines for schools

It is important that churches are aware of the needs of the primary school in relation to the School Standards scheme of work and the locally agreed RE syllabus. This may vary from local authority to local authority but all will encompass a programme of study that is broadly Christian. The events of Holy Week and Easter will undoubtedly be part of that programme and it is worth looking at a copy so that you are able to demonstrate to the school that the presentation is relevant and useful in delivering the curriculum. Most schools will be very grateful for the offer of the event but, if the area includes a variety of faith groups, the schools will need to know what is going to be covered. They may need to contact parents in order to reassure them that the story is part of the programme of study.

As always when dealing with schools, sensitivity is vital. Some team members may feel that this is an opportunity to evangelise, but the school is not the correct platform for doing so. Unlike the children who attend holiday clubs or lunchtime clubs, pupils are not choosing to come to the presentation; they are being brought as a class activity. It is important to keep a good relationship with the schools, so a professional approach to the material is an excellent witness, showing that the church recognises the needs of the pupils. Often, churches or Christian groups include primary school teachers among their members and advice from them would be helpful. For further information about the locally agreed syllabus, contact the Education Offices or RE adviser.

The Standards Site, www.standards.dfes.gov.uk, is useful for referencing topics likely to be in the school's scheme of work. For example, Attainment target 1 level 3 expects pupils to 'make links between beliefs and sources, including religious stories and sacred texts. They begin to identify the impact religion has on believers' lives. They describe some forms of religious expression.' Attainment target 2 level 4 expects children to 'raise, and suggest answers to, questions of identity, belonging, meaning, purpose, truth, values and commitments. They apply their ideas to their own and other people's lives.'

The experience of *The Easter Journey* enables pupils to consider the significance of the last days of Jesus' life for Christians and fulfils much of the work of Unit 4c: 'Why is Easter important for Christians?' It encourages pupils to reflect upon and ask questions about the reasons behind the festival. There are further appropriate links in the suggested schemes of work on the Standards Site, and the local authority agreed syllabus will be a useful source of comparison.

If funding allows, a small gift to each school, such as an assembly book, together with publicity material from reputable Christian publishers, is a tangible souvenir of the journey experience. (See www.barnabasinschools.org.uk for assembly resources.)

Learning outcomes

By the end of *The Easter Journey*, most children will be able to:

- Identify some of the significant parts of the Easter story.
- Place them in the context of Jesus' life and work.
- Ask questions about why Jesus came and what that means to believers.
- Make connections with the themes in the story and some of the core beliefs of Christianity.
- Make connections with some of the festivals and sacraments important in Christianity.

Considering learning styles

When developing *The Easter Journey*, much thought was given to the varied learning styles of children. It is now widely acknowledged that children learn in different ways. Some children prefer the experiential hands-on approach; others will appreciate storytelling; yet more will respond to entering into the life of a character and acting out a story. *The Easter Journey* is designed to appeal to a wide variety of learning styles so that there is inclusion for all. Children are invited to experience the journey through the five senses and also are asked to reflect on and wonder about the things they hear and see. Open-ended questions are important to help pupils to consider their thoughts and feelings. The scripts give suggestions and ideas, particularly for the final activity. For further information about mind-friendly learning and learning intelligences, see *Creating a Learning Church* by Margaret Cooling (Barnabas, 2005). Information is also widely available on the Internet.

Risk assessment

Many schools are now much more regulated about how children can be taken out of school. They need consent forms from parents or carers and will want to know more about the experience in which their children will be involved. A risk assessment needs to be done before each educational visit made by schools and, if the venue can provide a ready-made assessment for the experience, it will be helpful for the teacher organising the trip. This is not as onerous as it sounds. A sample is given on pages 46–47, although it would need to be tailored to be appropriate for an individual building.

*

Checklists

Three months to go

- Pray. Make prayer cards (see page 45).
- Decide on the format and leadership structure.
- If necessary, establish a working budget with the church treasurer. If the event is a joint effort, organisations such as Churches Together could be approached to assist.

Two months to go

- Assemble the team.
- Send publicity for event to other churches.
- Send invitations to schools and arrange timetable.
- Book transport (if required). Send an itinerary to coach firm when confirmed.

One month or less to go

- Organise team training.
- Allocate roles.
- Prepare the scenery, props, costumes and audio resources.
- Set up the venue.
- Ensure that toilet facilities are clearly labelled.
- Install lighting and video projection (if appropriate).
- Distribute labels, T-shirts or other 'uniform' items to the team.
- Carry out a risk assessment. Make sure that fire exits are clearly labelled.
- Walk through the experience for the whole team, with characters in place, so that everyone is familiar with the format.

During the event

- Pray at the beginning of each day.
- Confirm transport arrangements each morning (if possible, take the coach driver's mobile telephone number).
- Make sure each of the team members is in place. As mentioned, it is better that the team leader is not heavily involved with the presentation so that he or she is free to troubleshoot, network with staff and keep a general overview of timing and organisation.
- Make sure everyone knows who is in charge should there be an emergency and that procedures are in place to deal with it.
- Have a system for welcoming school parties, leaving coats, visiting toilets and so on.
- Provide refreshments for staff.
- Provide resources for staff to look through (if available). Barnabas promotional materials and publications can be easily obtained (see www.barnabasinschools.org.uk for details).
- Have a system for ensuring that, on leaving, each group receives books and so on.
- Enjoy the journey! You are sowing seeds that will grow and mature for God's kingdom.

*

Sample invitation

[Address of hosting church]
[date]

Dear [name of head teacher]

The churches of [name of town] would like to invite the children of [name of school] to take part in a presentation of *The Easter Journey*. This will be a free multimedia event involving drama, music, role-play and storytelling.

Pupils will experience eight scenes from the story in order to learn about the events of Holy Week and the first Easter, and explore its relevance today. The presentation will last for approximately one hour and is available for your Year 5 children. The event can take up to 30 children plus accompanying adults.

Either: The churches of [name of town] and [name of sponsor] have kindly agreed to provide coach transport from your school to and from the event.
Or: Coach travel can be arranged, if required, at a cost of around £ [cost].

The event will take place at [venue] on [date] and [date] to coincide with [related event if appropriate].

Older and younger children will have the chance to visit the event with their families on [date] from [time] onwards. We would be delighted if you could advertise this in your school newsletters. A flier will be sent separately.

We do hope that your children will be able to take part at the time offered below. Please could you let us know as soon as possible that you wish to accept the invitation and confirm the number of pupils and accompanying adults in your group. Please contact us if the given time or date is not convenient so that we can rearrange the time of your visit.

Date: Pick up time: Return time:

We will contact you by telephone before the event to confirm arrangements.

With best wishes

[name of leader(s)]
[contact telephone number(s)]
[contact email address(es)]

Sample prayer card

Please pray for *The Easter Journey*
On: _____
At: _____

- For everyone in the team.
- For a positive response from the schools.
- For the children and adults who come.
- For the evening/weekend journey for the public.
- That God will be glorified.

'These are things we learnt from our ancestors, and we will tell them to the next generation. We won't keep secret the glorious deeds and the mighty miracles of the Lord'
(Psalm 78:3–4).

Sample risk assessment form

Activity	Hazard	Who is at risk?	Level of risk			Control measures to be taken to reduce risk level to low Severity: S=1–4 (1=low); Likelihood: L=1–4; Risk: R=SxL	Controlled level of risk		
			S	L	R		S	L	R
The Easter Journey experience	Slips, trips and falls	All	1	2	2	Nobody may run around. Care to be taken when moving around the building. Adequate supervision of visitors to *The Easter Journey* by teachers and adults.	1	1	1
	Fire	All	1	2	2	No smoking allowed in the building. Sources of ignition must be kept under control. Hot objects must be supervised adequately (such as bulbs, lamps, bread-making equipment). Fire exits to be left clear and unobstructed.	1	1	1
	Electrical equipment	All	1	2	2	All electrical equipment to be electrically tested. Equipment used to be periodically checked during *The Easter Journey*. Cabling to be routed away from high-risk areas and covered with duct tape.	1	1	1

*

Sample risk assessment form

Hazard	Who at risk				Control measures			
Evacuation of building	All	1	3	3	Use of appropriate exits to be observed at all times. Fire exits to be left clear and unobstructed. In the event of evacuation, everyone to report to the car park for checking. Adequate supervision of visitors to make sure all are evacuated from building calmly and quietly and moved to a place of safety. In event of emergency help being needed, Main Street leaders to contact 999 by mobile phone.	1	2	2
Unloading and loading of buses	Pupils and school staff	2	3	6	Adequate supervision of pupils by teachers and other adults.	1	2	2
Trapping fingers in doors	All	2	2	4	Adequate supervision by teachers and other adults. Pupils given warning about the doors.	1	2	2

Compiled by [name of compiler] [date]

*

Creating the journey

As we have seen, after the introductory warm-up, the children are led around eight scenes designed to help them to experience some of the significant events of Holy Week and Easter from a biblical perspective. The whole picture is based on the Christian belief in God's rescue plan for the world and follows on from *The Christmas Journey*, which, ideally, the children will have experienced in Year 2 (although this is not an essential requirement). For Christians, Jesus' death and resurrection are central to faith but, for various reasons, contemporary culture has diminished the importance of Easter to no more than an extra Bank Holiday involving a great deal of chocolate. Consequently, many pupils come to the journey with less knowledge of the Easter stories than of Christmas.

The Easter Journey relates the story of the final days of Jesus' life by creating an interactive storyboard, with each scene chosen to reflect both its place in the big picture and also the everyday situations in which the biblical characters found themselves. Jesus is portrayed as the king for whom the Jewish people were waiting, but also the king who surprised and confused them. Pupils are given an opportunity at the end of the journey to reflect on the things they have seen and heard.

It is very important to create a smooth transition from scene to scene, allowing for a sense of mystery and suspense as the children travel together from one area to the next as a whole class. Within the large group, small groups relate to a leader who is trained to link areas together and to encourage pupils to participate in the different experiences they encounter. The children meet characters and storytellers as they travel from scene to scene and they take part in role-play and discussion.

The Easter Journey is designed to appeal to differing learning styles. A multisensory approach enables pupils to respond in their own way. Using a combination of touch, smell, taste, listening, drama and role-play, each of the scenes stimulates children's imaginations and helps them respond to the story. The scenes chosen are:

- Palm Sunday
- In the temple
- The stone that the builders rejected
- The last supper
- The garden of Gethsemane
- The crucifixion
- The day in between
- The resurrection garden

The eight scenes are preceded by a warm-up to introduce the story, and there is an opportunity to reflect on the experience at the conclusion of the journey.

The set

Sets and props can be as simple or elaborate as desired, depending on the skills and talents available. Much will depend on the facilities and amount of space in the building. The church in Frodsham is fortunate to have a square worship area that can be completely cleared of furniture to accommodate three square pop-up dark green gazebos to act as the rooms for the last supper and the 'day in between' scenes. It is worth buying or borrowing good-quality metal gazebos if you plan to repeat the event, as plastic ones are more complicated to erect and less robust for attaching drapes. Gazebos are ideal as they are easy to assemble, take little room for storage after the event and can be adapted by removing or adding sides, drapes and hangings.

It is worth thinking creatively about the use of space and possibilities for doubling up areas. For example, the church at

Frodsham has a large hall, suitable for the first part of the story, and a lounge area that links the two main areas and is used for the story of the stone that the builders rejected. This latter area is then transformed into the resurrection garden. Using gazebos in the main worship area for Scenes 4 and 7 leaves the rest of the space free for the garden of Gethsemane and the crucifixion scene. The children move back into the first area for the discussion and conclusion of the experience.

If your space is large or has fixed furniture, it may be possible to create smaller areas using screens, wood or even corrugated cardboard. Imaginative use of fabrics and lighting can hide a multitude of distractions. Large quantities of dark fabrics can be purchased very cheaply from discount textile warehouses, curtain shops and so on. It is worth trying to obtain fabric that will not fray or need ironing so that it can be easily cut and reused.

It is important to arrange a smooth transition from scene to scene in order to keep the children focused on the story. If necessary, link areas together using screens or drapes to create a passageway effect, allowing children to move freely through the journey without distraction. Fabric can be stapled to slats of wood, which can then be secured to screens or gazebos with strong string. Take care that wood is safely fastened in order to prevent accidents. Ask the children to take care when moving around. The nature of the journey is such that children are rarely distracted and respond very positively to moving from area to area in a mysterious and anticipatory manner.

The suggested room plan for *The Easter Journey* can be found on page 121 and on the website, www.easterjourney.org.uk. Photos of the event can also be accessed on the website.

Lighting

Lighting plays a vital role in creating an intimate atmosphere in each setting. It is easy to create a professional effect with simple lighting, readily available in local furniture and DIY stores. Free-standing uplighters, clip-on spotlights and battery-operated nightlights and lanterns can all be used to good effect. It may be possible to hire or borrow more professional lighting systems but this is not strictly necessary. Care needs to be taken with hiding wires and adapters. Photos and diagrams on the website show the set-up that was used in Frodsham, but much will depend on what is available and the proximity to electrical sockets in your building. Although some of the areas should be as dark as possible, attention to health and safety is paramount and, for this reason, background lighting is advisable.

Part Two

The Easter Journey

*

Introductory warm-up

As previously mentioned, it is important that there is a smooth transition from scene to scene so that the whole experience runs seamlessly. Encourage group leaders to keep in role at all times to enable the children and helpers to take part in a thoughtful and focused way.

On arrival, the children are welcomed to the presentation and are told that they are going on a very special journey. They are invited into the first space and are greeted by the storyteller, who introduces him- or herself. The storyteller asks the children to join him or her on a very special journey at this special time of year.

Handy hint
Throughout the presentation, it is important to remember that children are used to drama and role-play as part of their everyday curriculum. A firm but friendly manner and high expectation of behaviour helps to establish boundaries with lively Year 5s. Teachers are there to supervise if needed, but it is also helpful if they are encouraged to join in the experience.

Aim

To introduce the children to the storyteller and other team members; to introduce the story of Easter and the *Easter Journey* presentation, and to help children settle into the environment.

Setting the scene

The warm-up helps the children to understand that Jerusalem, at this point in history, was a place full of contradictions. It was ruled by the Romans and security was high because of the approaching

Passover festival. Many travellers had come to the city to take part in the festival and the streets were crowded. Jesus entered this busy scene riding on a donkey—not at all what would be expected of a king. His reputation as a teacher, healer and worker of miracles had gone before him and there was much excitement and anticipation at his arrival. The children are asked to imagine how they would have felt, being part of that crowd.

Character(s)

- Storyteller

Costume

- None

Scenery

No scenery is necessary, just a space large enough for the children to move around. No special lighting is needed other than a feeling of daylight.

Props

- None

Handy hint
If space allows, rather than miming on the spot, invite the children to wander about and capture in freeze-poses the moods of that week—such as excitement, surprise, suspicion, fear, sadness, puzzlement, disbelief, shock and so on.

Script: Introductory warm-up

Storyteller: We are about to set out on a journey. We are going to travel through the days that led up to what we now know as Easter Day. They are dramatic days. There will be lots to see and do and touch and taste and feel. We want to try to work out for ourselves what we think this journey means for us today. The Easter story has meant a great deal to people down the ages and has even changed their lives. However, it has to be a story we work out for ourselves. I wonder what this Easter journey will mean for you today.

To go on our Easter journey, we need to step into a story. In fact, we are following in the footsteps of Jesus and his friends in the most dramatic week of Jesus' life. Let's get ourselves ready to step into the story of Jesus' Easter journey.

During this week we will experience many different moods. Some people have walked for miles to be in Jerusalem for the great festival of Passover *(start miming walking on the spot, and encourage the children to join in)*.

It was a week that began with processions and people running to join the crowds *(mime running and jostling, but don't allow the children to push each other)*.

But in the narrow streets of Jerusalem you could not move quickly *(mime people shuffling along)*.

And with such large crowds there were security fears, so there were soldiers about *(mime marching on the spot)*.

It was a week full of highs and lows, hopes and fears. Sometimes in the story people thought it best just to creep quietly around in the dark *(mime creeping quietly)*.

It was a week that ended in a most unexpected way. People began running about again because they discovered something that changes everything *(mime running in excitement)*.

What they heard and what they saw stunned people and left many rooted to the spot *(mime standing stock still)*.

So are you ready? Let's step into the story of the Easter journey!

Staying in the same room or area, the storyteller leads the children straight into the next story.

✳

Scene 1

Palm Sunday

———————— Bible background ————————
Matthew 21:1–11; Mark 11:1–11; Luke 19:28–38;
John 12:12–15

Aim

To introduce the idea that the people were looking for a special person or leader, perhaps a king, who would lead them against the Romans and restore their country. However, they began to realise that Jesus was not that kind of king. What sort of king is Jesus? He is an unexpected king!

Setting the scene

Encourage the children to role-play the part of the crowds who welcomed Jesus into the city of Jerusalem.

Characters

- Storyteller
- Helpers join in the role-play to give a lead to the children.

Costume

- None

Scenery

- None

Props

- Coconut shells to sound like donkey's hooves
- An imitation microphone to use for interviews

Script: Palm Sunday

Storyteller: It all began on a Sunday, the first day of the week. Rumours were flying around (*encourage the children to whisper to each other*).

Jesus was arriving for the festival. Jesus said such wonderful things and did such amazing things that people always looked forward to his arrival. Somehow, whenever he turned up, unexpected things happened. Some people were even saying he was the new king, the one they were all expecting—the Messiah. They were hoping that he would rescue them from the Romans (*encourage the children to boo or hiss*).

Suddenly people heard the news that Jesus was arriving soon via the gate into the city known as Sheep Gate. The crowds rushed to line the streets (*arrange the children in two lines*).

Everyone strained to see what was happening (*mime straining to see*).

Was he coming? Was that him? Hope was in the air (*encourage general excitement*).

Suddenly, people caught sight of Jesus in the distance. A cloud of dust… that must be him! Everyone began to shout and cheer *(encourage the children to cheer)*.

Someone had a good idea. Why not welcome him like a real king and wave palm branches? They climbed the trees and cut down branches. Other people took off their outer cloaks and laid them on the road, so that Jesus would have a sort of royal carpet to tread on *(encourage the children to either mime waving palm branches or to pretend to take off an outer garment and lay it on the road)*.

Everyone wanted a king who would rescue them from the Roman army, so they began calling out 'Rescue us', which in their language is 'Hosanna!' *(encourage the children to call out 'Hosanna!)*.

Suddenly, a sound could be heard… it was the sound of donkey's hooves *(use coconuts to make the sound and encourage the children to look to the top of the room as if watching to see Jesus enter)*.

The shouting died down *(encourage the children to be quiet)*. But what was this? What was Jesus riding? A donkey? That was no way for a king to arrive. Surely he should be on a horse! A big, powerful horse would be much more suitable for a king!

Freeze the scene and 'interview' some of the children using the microphone.

> What sort of king do you think Jesus is? What sort of person was God sending to rescue his people? What would you have expected Jesus to do? *(Encourage role-play answers from several children.)*

*

In the temple

——————————— Bible background ———————————
Matthew 21:12–13; Mark 11:15–18; Luke 19:45–46

Aim

To show the children that Jesus was not afraid to upset people who were not following God's way. He was not a king who would be influenced by popularity, but would challenge the status quo if necessary. What sort of king is Jesus? He is a disturbing king!

Setting the scene

After his entry into the city, Jesus visited the temple. The outer courts of the temple had become a market place for traders cashing in on the pilgrims visiting Jerusalem. There were people selling animals and birds, which would then be offered to God as a peace-offering, and money changers charging too much for people to exchange Roman coins for temple money. The temple—God's house—had become a noisy place of dishonest trading rather than a quiet place of worship. Using the same space as before, the children are asked to play the part of the traders in the temple and enter into the drama of the event.

Character(s)

- Storyteller (It is preferable for continuity if the storyteller is the same person as before, although it is possible to use a second person if necessary.)

Costume

- None

Scenery

- None

Props

- Three large cardboard cartons, about 1m high, to act as stalls for the traders. These are easily obtained from office suppliers and can be strengthened with parcel tape. They do not need to be decorated; they are simply representational.

Script: In the temple

Divide the children into three groups, each gathered around a cardboard carton. The groups become some of the sellers in the marketplace of the temple. They each have their own 'group shout', such as:

- 'Sheep, sheep, two for the price of one!'
- 'Pigeons, pigeons, get your pigeons here!'
- 'Money, money, change your money now!' (or 'at our special rates!')

Invite the children to suggest some appropriate actions, such as scurrying feet when Jesus turns over the tables. The storyteller should build up the drama of this scene by encouraging the children to shout out their wares, first one group, then adding the second and finally the third as the chorus of voices grows louder. The leaders encourage their groups to shout out loudly above the others.

The storyteller, acting as Jesus, ends the commotion by indicating for the children to stop shouting.

Storyteller: Stop! God's house should be a place of worship, but you have turned it into a place where robbers hide!

The storyteller (carefully) tips over the boxes and pretends to scatter each of the groups. He or she then asks the children to freeze in a moment of shock and surprise. The storyteller uses the microphone again to 'interview' the groups, asking what they think has happened. What do the children think of Jesus now? What sort of king do they think he is?

*

Scene 3

The stone that the builders rejected

————————— Bible background —————————
Matthew 21:33–46; Mark 12:1–12; Luke 20:9–19;
Psalm 118:22

Aim

To familiarise pupils with one of the stories Jesus told during the week that has come to be known as Holy Week; to help them understand that Jesus often used stories with hidden meanings (parables) to explain things about God; to enable children to imagine for themselves what the story might mean. What sort of king is Jesus? An unwanted and a suffering king.

Setting the scene

During the days leading up to the Passover festival, Jesus spent time talking to people, healing those who were unwell and telling stories. He challenged the teaching of the chief priests and leaders who were by now questioning his authority and feeling concerned about his influence on ordinary people.

The story of the tenants in the vineyard tells of a land owner who puts his tenants in charge of his vineyard while he goes on a journey. He sends back servants to get some of the harvest, but they are killed by the tenants. Eventually, the owner sends his son, who is also taken and killed. Jesus asks those who are listening what they think the owner will do. He goes on to talk about the stone that the builders rejected becoming the most important stone of all. In saying this, he is warning the chief priests and leaders that God will not allow his kingdom to be ruled by those who do not do as he commands. Many people were puzzled by what Jesus said, but the chief priests and leaders knew that Jesus was talking about them.

Character(s)

* Storyteller (This can be the same person as before or a different person, if desired.)

Costume

* None

Scenery

There is no need for scenery in the story, although it is preferable if the children are taken to a different room from the first area, where everything is ready for them. In the presentation in Frodsham, the same (second) room is used subsequently for the resurrection garden scene, so the room is dressed as a garden, but the scenery is disguised with greenery, and a piece of hardboard, painted to resemble a bush, covers the tomb. (Flowers are added to transform the scene into the resurrection garden, so they are not present when the children first enter the room.)

Props

Some large pebbles are provided in baskets for the children to handle, and a large rectangular piece of rock sits in the middle of the room. The storyteller uses pebbles to create a wall effect for the vineyard.

Script: The stone that the builders rejected

Invite the children to sit down in the room, which is scattered with pebbles. In the middle of the room is the large rectangular rock. The pebbles become the prompt for one of the stories that Jesus told during that last week of his Easter journey

Storyteller: Many strange things happened during the next days. Jesus and his friends stayed in a village outside the city, near to a hill called the Mount of Olives. Each morning Jesus would go into the city and join with the festival crowds and then, near to the temple, he would sit down and tell stories.

The temple was a magnificent building. It had taken years and years to build. It shone with its gold decorations. Its beautiful carved stonework gleamed in the sunlight, its towers and columns were overpowering in their splendour. In fact, the temple was still in the process of being built and there were stones lying around which the builders had rejected. It was near these that Jesus once told a very special story.

Encourage the children to pick up the stones and feel them.

Just think how old the stones in our story might have been. How far might they have come? They would have been cut from quarries, chipped and shaped to become part of the magnificent temple.

But not every stone had been used. There was one stone in particular that caught Jesus' eye.

Draw the children's attention to the big stone. Feel its shape as the story begins to unfold.

Jesus pointed out that this was one of the stones that the builders had rejected. I wonder what they didn't like about it. I wonder why they decided they couldn't use it. Was it the wrong shape? Wouldn't it fit? Didn't they like its colour? It made Jesus think of a song from the Psalms. Jesus looked up and remembered words he learned when he was very young: 'The stone that the builders tossed aside is now the most important stone of all.'

Invite the children to touch and handle the stones. Ask them to look out for 'building' words during the story, and, of course, to watch out for the mention of stones.

Let me tell you a story to show you what Jesus meant.

There was once a landowner who planted a vineyard. He wanted grapes to grow so that he could make some fine wine. He called in the builders to make a strong wall right around his land to keep the vineyard safe.

Make an outline with the stones.

He got his men to dig a ditch to keep out the wild animals. He even prepared a great vat in which they could collect the grapes once they'd grown, to crush them for the juice to make the wine. This was his own vineyard, his special place.

Finally, he had one more building put up. On the edge of the vineyard he built a great tower, a watchtower to make sure no enemies came to steal the grapes.

Build a small tower with stones at one corner of the vineyard.

He did everything possible to make sure of a good harvest. Then the landowner had to go on a journey, so he left some hired servants to look after the vineyard in his absence. But he had to be away longer than he planned and he couldn't be there when the harvest time came.

The landowner sent some messengers to go and bring back a share of the harvest so that he could at least taste the fine grapes that he had planted.

When those messengers arrived at the vineyard, the hired servants decided they would not give up what they'd been looking after. They wanted the vineyard for themselves. Instead of giving the messengers some of the harvest, they told them to go away. They beat them up, chased them away and sent them packing. When the owner got to hear what was happening, he sent some more messengers, but they too were badly treated. The servants even killed one of the messengers and threw stones at others so that none dared go near the vineyard. Every group that the owner sent was treated in the same terrible way.

Finally, the owner decided to send his own son to the vineyard. 'They won't dare to treat him badly,' he thought. 'They will respect him. They will hand over some of the grapes to him so he can bring them back to me.'

When the hired servants saw the son coming, they began to plot. 'This is the owner's son,' they thought. 'It will all be his one day. But if we got rid of him, then the vineyard could truly be ours.' So they ganged up on him. They grabbed him. They dragged him outside the vineyard and... they killed him.

Bring one of the stones crashing down on to the large rectangular stone to indicate the moment of the son's death.

The crowds near Jesus gasped. What a terrible story! Even as they were thinking that, Jesus asked a question. 'When the owner of that vineyard comes, what do you suppose he will do to those tenants?' he asked.

Invite some responses from the children.

> You're right. They deserve to be put to death. The vineyard doesn't belong to the likes of them. They have rejected the owner's only son. But listen…

Hold on to the big stone.

> 'The stone that the builders tossed aside is now the most important stone of all.'
>
> I wonder what Jesus was talking about. What has this got to do with Jesus' Easter journey? Many people in the crowd were puzzled… but some of them realised what the story was really about.

✶

Scene 4

The last supper

———————— Bible background ————————
Matthew 26:26–30; Mark 14:22–26; Luke 22:14–23;
John 13:1–7

Aim

To help pupils to experience the story of the last supper that Jesus shared with his disciples. This story is linked with the idea of Jesus serving his disciples by washing their feet. What sort of king is Jesus? A servant king and a mysterious king.

Setting the scene

Jesus and the disciples were in the city of Jerusalem to celebrate the Passover festival. The sacrament or special ritual that we now know as the Holy Communion is based on the things Jesus did and said at this meal. The meal took the form of the traditional Passover meal in which the Jewish people remembered how, led by Moses, the Israelites escaped from Pharaoh's Egypt after the angel of death had 'passed over' their houses. All the elements of the meal have meaning for Jewish people. A special plate called a *Seder* plate is used, which holds seven foods, all with symbolic meaning.

- A lamb bone represents the lamb sacrificed on the last night.
- Bitter herbs remind the people of the bitter time as slaves in Egypt.
- Salt water represents the tears of the slaves.
- Unleavened bread (bread without yeast) is used as there was no time for the bread to rise on the night when the slaves escaped.

- Charoset (a mixture of apple, cinnamon, nuts and wine) symbolises the mortar holding together the bricks that the slaves had to make.
- Roasted egg represents their new life after leaving Egypt.
- Parsley and spring onion provide a sign of new life.

Traditionally, the youngest child in the family asks the question, 'What makes this night so special?'

Jesus arranged to eat the Passover meal with his disciples in an upper room in the city.

Characters

- Jesus and Peter
- Storyteller
- The youngest child (arrange previously with the teacher to ensure that the youngest child in the group is happy to read a sentence)

Costume

Jesus and Peter are both dressed in modern dress, such as white T-shirts and jeans.

Scenery

Two gazebos are placed side by side, with an adjoining open side, to create a large room. The lighting is dim and the walls are plain, created from either the sides of the gazebos or dark fabric and screens.

Props

- Low tables are placed in the centre of the room to create a table long enough for the children to sit round, either on the floor or on cushions. The table is covered in a white cloth.
- A *Seder* plate is placed in the middle of the table with the following items in place: lamb bone, herbs, salt water, matzo bread, charoset, hard-boiled egg and spring onions.

- Battery-operated tealight candles help to give atmosphere, and there are pottery jugs and beakers to represent the wine.
- Wooden plates of matzo bread and dishes of grapes complete the table setting. There should be enough plates of matzo and grapes to pass round to everyone.
- A large pitcher and a towel are placed near where Jesus is to sit.
- Battery-operated garden lanterns are also useful to provide the appropriate atmosphere. For safety reasons, real candles or oil lights should not be used.

For suppliers of *Seder* plates and battery-operated tealight candles, see page 124. Alternatively, a large platter or tray can be used, with small dishes containing the food items. It may be possible to borrow a *Seder* plate from the RE department of a local secondary school. Some primary schools also have their own artefacts.

Script: The last supper

The groups are led quietly into the darkened room and the children are encouraged to sit down on the floor around the table. Jesus and Peter are already sitting centrally at the table, ready to mime the story. Group leaders explain to the children quietly that they are invited to take part in the meal. The children are offered a piece of matzo bread and a grape. Once all the children are settled and have taken some food, the narrator begins to read.

Storyteller: On the Thursday of that week, Jesus' Easter journey takes us to an upstairs room in a street in the city of Jerusalem, where Jesus was eating a special meal with his friends. When everyone had settled at the table, Jesus got up. He tied a towel around his waist and fetched a jug of water and a bowl. He began to wash the dust from his friends' feet.

Jesus mimes washing Peter's feet.

The table was set with special food. There was lamb to eat and some flat bread that had not risen in the way that the bread we buy in the shops does. This flat bread is called unleavened bread. Then the youngest person in the room spoke up.

Youngest child: What makes this night so special?

Storyteller: Jesus told his friends that they were celebrating how God had rescued his people from slavery and brought them through the waters of the Red Sea to freedom.

God had told the people to sprinkle the blood of a lamb on their doorposts. The angel of death would see the blood and pass over their homes. They had to get ready to travel so they quickly baked bread for their journey. There was no time to let the bread rise.

At the end of the meal, Jesus took a piece of the flat bread. He said 'thank you' to God and then he broke the bread and handed it to his friends with the words, 'This is my body, which is given for you. Eat this as a way of remembering me!'

Jesus mimes this action.

> Then Jesus poured out some more wine and said to his friends, 'This is my blood. It is poured out for you, and with it God makes his new agreement.'

Jesus mimes this action.

> Whatever did Jesus mean? What was he talking about? Jesus was always saying puzzling things.

> After this, Judas, one of Jesus' friends, slipped out of the room. When the meal was finished, everyone sang a hymn. Then Jesus led them out into the night. *(Jesus leaves the room with Peter.)* They went to a garden beneath the city walls, where Jesus wanted to pray.

After Jesus has left the room, the group leaders tell the children that they are going to follow Jesus into the garden. They encourage the children to creep quietly through the doorway into the next scene.

*

The garden of Gethsemane

————————— Bible background —————————
Matthew 26:36–56; Mark 14:32–50; Luke 22:39–53;
John 18:1–12

Aim

To help pupils understand what happened in the garden of
Gethsemane; to help the children experience how Jesus was arrested
and how he and the disciples felt at this time. What sort of king is
Jesus? A captured king and a lonely king.

Setting the scene

After the Passover meal, Jesus asked his disciples to go with him to
the garden of Gethsemane. When they got there, he left them for a
while so that he could be alone to pray. The disciples did not fully
understand the danger that Jesus was now in and they fell asleep.
Earlier, Jesus had warned them that one of them would betray him,
but they had all vehemently denied it. Late into the night, Judas led
a mob, assembled by the chief priests and leaders, to arrest Jesus.
Jesus was taken away to be tried by Caiaphas the high priest and,
subsequently, by Pontius Pilate, the Roman governor.

Character(s)

• None: the whole scene is based on a listening experience so
  that the children use their imaginations to understand what is
  happening.

Costume

- None

Scenery

The children are led into a darkened area where they are asked to crouch behind bushes made from plywood and listen to the noises of the night. If possible, a painted scene of the distant city at night could be the focal point. Many Christmas cards show scenes of a Middle Eastern town, and a scene like this can be copied from a card on to corrugated cardboard and stapled to a wooden frame. Alternatively, the scene can be traced on to a piece of acetate and projected on to a large piece of card. The outline can then be drawn and painted with poster or emulsion paint. Dark buildings and lighted windows give the impression of a night scene.

Props

Stylised bushes can be made using plywood cut into simple bush-like shapes, then slotted together (see www.easterjourney.org.uk for reference). The bushes should be 80 to 100cm high and about 150cm wide. You will need six bushes spaced evenly around the area, allowing up to five children to hide behind each bush. You will also need a CD of sound effects, which can be recorded live or downloaded from the Internet. For further details, see the website www.easterjourney.org.uk. The CD needs to include night sounds (cicadas and so on) to provide a continuous background beneath the following sequence of sounds:

- Walking in the undergrowth
- A person walking alone
- Sighing
- A voice whispering the words 'Do what you want, and not what I want.'

- People sleeping
- Marching feet coming closer
- A scuffle and raised voices
- A sword fight
- Footsteps running away
- Soldiers marching away
- Quiet night sounds
- A cock crowing

The whole sequence should last no longer than five minutes. If you have difficulty in putting the CD together, you could consider approaching a local secondary school or FE college, where the project could be undertaken by a media student. As well as the sound effects CD, suitable dramatic music playing softly in the background can give a sense of continuity to the experience. The soundtrack to the film *The Lion, the Witch and the Wardrobe* has some excellent tracks. Track 11, 'The Stone Table', is very suitable as background music in this scene.

Lighting

It is important to provide atmospheric lighting to create a sense of mystery and anticipation. Although the scene takes place at night, there does need to be some ambient light in order for the children to see where they are. Also, group leaders may find lanterns or torches useful. If professional lighting is used, a moon projected on to the scenery can give enough light for the safe movement of the children. Also, coloured acetate sheets can be used in front of spotlights to create a sense of foreboding.

Script: The garden of Gethsemane

There is no script as such for this scene because it is based on listening to sound effects.

Jesus asks the children to follow him to the garden as he leaves the previous scene (the last supper). Group leaders allow Jesus and Peter time to get out of the way before they usher the children into the next space. It could be useful for the person playing the part of Jesus to go behind the scenery to switch on the CD, once the children are settled behind the bushes. The leaders help the children to hide in the space and encourage them to listen carefully to the sounds so that they can work out what is happening. The scene does not require too much explanation from leaders as it is revisited later in the journey.

The sound effects CD lasts for about five minutes and experience shows that the children readily take part in the adventure, entering into it with imagination and enthusiasm. Leaders can encourage the children to question what they have heard but hold on to those thoughts until the end of the journey. Once the sound effects of the garden have ended, leaders ask the children to move out of the bushes towards the other side of the room for the next part of the story.

✳

Scene 6

The crucifixion

—————————— Bible background ——————————
Matthew 26:47—27:66; Mark 14:43—15:41;
Luke 22:47—23:49; John 18:1—19:37

Aim

To familiarise pupils with the story of Jesus' trial and crucifixion; to help the children understand the effect that this had on those who loved him and followed him. What sort of king is Jesus? A king who had to die.

Setting the scene

After the scene in the garden of Gethsemane, Jesus was arrested and taken to the high priest, Caiaphas. Together with the priests and leaders, Caiaphas tried to find evidence of Jesus' blasphemy. Eventually, after some plotting, they decided that Jesus should be put to death. He was taken to Pilate, the Roman governor, to sanction the death sentence. Meanwhile, Peter told some people who recognised him that he had not been with Jesus.

Pilate could find no case against Jesus and tried to persuade the Jewish people to let him go, using the Passover tradition of setting free a prisoner. However, the leaders persuaded the crowd to turn against Jesus and, in spite of his misgivings, Pilate agreed with the sentence. The scene was set for the ultimate penalty: a painful death on a wooden cross.

Characters

- Storyteller (prerecorded on to a DVD)
- Mary, mother of Jesus
- Peter

Costume

- Mary is dressed in traditional Eastern dress, very much in the style seen in nativity pictures.
- Peter wears a simple white T-shirt and jeans, or similar.

Scenery

- A plain unadorned space, adjacent to the garden of Gethsemane scene.

Props

- A screen with good visibility for the children.
- A DVD of images, sounds and readings, telling the story of the crucifixion (see suggested script on the following pages). Some ideas for reflections about the crucifixion are also available on the website www.easterjourney.org.uk and through other sources, such as Lifewords.
- DVD or video projector and a compatible computer (for the presentation).

Lighting

The area needs to be dark for most of the time. A spotlight should be trained on the place where Mary and Peter speak. A domestic spotlight with a dimmer switch would be suitable. However, if a professional follow spot can be obtained, this adds atmosphere to the drama of the scene. Professional spots can often be borrowed from a local secondary school or hired from a theatrical lighting company.

Script: The crucifixion

The children are asked to move from the bushes and sit in a space near the screen. Gaffer or masking tape can be used to define the sitting area so that children do not encroach on the actors. Once the children are settled, the DVD is started.

The DVD comprises the following narration, accompanied by sounds and images.

Storyteller: Many of the Jewish people were amazed at the things Jesus said and did, and they believed in him. The chief priests and nation's leaders were very jealous of Jesus. They called a meeting at the home of Caiaphas, the high priest, and secretly planned to have Jesus arrested and put to death.

'What do we do now?' they asked. 'If we let Jesus continue, pretty soon everyone will be believing in him and the Romans will come and take away what little power and privilege we still have.'

Judas Iscariot, one of the twelve disciples, went to the chief priests and asked, 'How much will you give me if I help you arrest Jesus?' They paid Judas 30 silver coins and from then on he started looking for a good chance to betray Jesus.

A few days later, late at night, Jesus was alone with his friends in the garden of Gethsemane. Judas arrived with a mob of armed soldiers sent by the priests. He had told them beforehand, 'Arrest the man I greet with a kiss.' Judas walked right up to Jesus and said, 'Hello, teacher!' Then Judas kissed him and the men grabbed Jesus and arrested him.

Jesus was led off to the high priest. Then the chief priests and the nation's leaders tried to find someone to accuse Jesus of a crime, so that they could put him to death. Finally, some men stood up and lied about him. The high priest stood up in the council and asked Jesus, 'Why don't you say something in your own defence? Don't you hear the charges they are making against you?' But Jesus kept quiet and did not say a word. The high priest asked him another question: 'Are you the Messiah, the Son of the glorious God?' 'Yes, I am!' Jesus answered. At once the high priest ripped his robe apart and shouted, 'Why do we need more witnesses? You heard him claim to be God! What is your decision?'

They tied up Jesus and led him off to Pilate, the Roman governor. Pilate questioned Jesus but could find nothing wrong. Pilate knew that the chief priests had brought Jesus to him because they were jealous of his popularity, but, not wanting to cause trouble, Pilate sentenced Jesus to death. He ordered his soldiers to beat Jesus with a whip and nail him to a cross.

The soldiers made fun of Jesus and led him off to be nailed to a cross. At midday the sky turned dark and stayed that way until the middle of the afternoon. The sun stopped shining, and the curtain in the temple split down the middle. Jesus shouted, 'Father, I put myself in your hands!' Then he died.

When the DVD ends, a spotlight highlights Mary, who walks in slowly from the side. She stands near the screen and delivers her script with overwhelming sadness.

Mary: What have they done to my son? Why did they have to be so cruel?

Oh God, how could you let this happen? I trusted you! I trusted you and it came to this. Oh, my son, why have you had to die in this way?

When I think back to the terrible journey to Bethlehem before you were born… and having to run away to Egypt to escape from King Herod when you were a tiny baby… Remember how we thought we'd lost you that time in Jerusalem when you were only twelve years old?

All the wonderful things you did. You healed those who were unwell; you cured those who could not walk; you gave sight to those who could not see. How could it come to this?

So many people will remember what you did in your life... how you taught us about your Father God and helped us to understand about his kingdom.

I never thought it would be like this. I knew it would come, but, oh... it's so hard.

Oh Jesus, my son, I will miss you so much. God, why did this have to happen? It's so final.

Mary quietly leaves as the spotlight fades. After a short space of time, Peter enters and the spotlight is brightened again.

Peter: I'm a fisherman. I used to think a night at sea in a bad storm with no fish was bad enough. I thought I'd left that behind when I met Jesus. But now... I'm not sure... I'm so confused. Jesus is gone. They killed him. Three years of my life, everything I believed in... gone! I believed in Jesus. I gave up my home and my job. I left my family and joined him. The more I heard him speak, the more I saw what he did, the more certain I was that Jesus was special. I'll never forget the day that I suddenly realised so clearly... so clearly... that he was the Son of God. He was the one we had been waiting for. The one people had said would lead us to freedom. *He* was the one... but now he's gone... he's dead. I'm so confused. What did I do wrong?

Last week, everyone was cheering and shouting when we came into Jerusalem. What a day that was—everyone wanting to get close, everyone wanting to be involved. You should have been there! The next day, Jesus really upset the temple leaders, throwing the market traders out and upsetting the money changers. He seemed so angry, but people really approved of what he did. You should have seen the way he did it. You'd have loved it!

And then, at the Passover meal, while we were celebrating the way that God rescued our ancestors from slavery in Egypt, Jesus washing our feet and telling us to remember him as a servant. That was a strange but special time. He ate with us, washed our feet and then gave us bread and wine to remember him by. If you'd been there, you'd never forget.

I can't believe it's been just one day since we ate that special meal with Jesus. After the meal, we went to his favourite place—the garden outside the city. I wish I had stayed awake when Jesus went off to pray, but I didn't. And then the guards came to arrest him… that woke us up! I wanted to fight, to protect him, but Jesus stopped me. I'm sure we could have escaped, but he let them take him away.

They took him to the high priest's house. They were all waiting for him in the middle of the night. I followed. I wanted to see what was happening, see what Jesus would do. I wanted to be there. I was like a spy following right into the enemy camp, trying to keep away from the guards. It was there I said three times that I didn't know Jesus. How could I have said such a thing? But there was danger all around me. Jesus couldn't have heard me, he was too far away, but he turned and looked me straight in the eye. I knew I had let him down, denied him, betrayed him. I got really scared then and ran away.

As that dreadful night turned into dawn, I learnt that they had dragged Jesus in front of Caiaphas, the high priest, and then Pontius Pilate, the Roman governor. Troublemakers had stirred up the crowd and they were condemning Jesus to death. Pilate had handed him to the soldiers to be taken away. That was all before nine o'clock in the morning.

I heard that some of the women had seen Jesus die. The soldiers had beaten Jesus, and then they had killed him by hanging him on a cross. It was the middle of the afternoon when Jesus died, and there could be no mistaking that he was dead. The women saw his body taken down, wrapped in cloth and placed in a grave. It was a cave dug into the hillside with the entrance closed by a huge stone. I don't even know who owned the grave.

This is the worst day of my life. I did nothing. I just allowed it to happen. And now it's all over. I can't believe it's happened. I'm afraid the guards will come for me.

Somehow, I thought Jesus would always be with me, but that can't happen... can it? I want to leave Jerusalem... perhaps I should go back to fishing. I can't believe what's happened.

Peter exits slowly as the spotlight fades.

Depending on the attention span of the children, it may be necessary to shorten Peter's script, but the important elements of the story need to be retained. After a short space of time for reflection, the original storyteller appears from the direction in which Peter and Mary left. He asks the children to follow him quietly.

*

Scene 7

The day in between

―――――――――――― Bible background ――――――――――――
Matthew 27:57–66; Mark 15:42–47; Luke 23:50–56; John 19:38–42

Aim

To explain to the children what happened after the crucifixion and how Jesus' body was placed in a borrowed tomb, sealed with a large stone. This scene is a very short but necessary experience, linking the darkness of the previous story to the light of Easter Day.

Setting the scene

After Jesus' death, Joseph of Arimathea, a respected Jewish leader, asked Pilate for the body. Along with Nicodemus, Joseph was a secret follower of Jesus. He had Jesus' body prepared for burial with spices and linen cloths and placed it in his own new tomb. He rolled a stone in front of it. The women watched as this happened, but there is no mention of the male disciples. The despair that they all felt can only be imagined. However, the chief priests still remembered how Jesus had prophesied that he would rise after three days, so Pilate ordered a watch to be put on the tomb in order to prevent false claims by Jesus' followers.

Characters

• Storyteller

Costume

• None

Scenery

A darkened bare space. A gazebo with dark walls can be used as a tunnel between the crucifixion scene and the resurrection garden. The children will only be standing in the space for a short time while the storyteller explains what happened on 'the day in between' but it is important that there are no distractions so that they get the idea of being suspended in time after the drama of the crucifixion.

Props

• None

Lighting

This should be as dim as is safely possible.

Script: The day in between

As previously mentioned, the storyteller appears after Peter has left the crucifixion scene. He or she invites the children to come into the darkened room.

Storyteller: Today everything has gone quiet, as we await the greatest event in the whole history of time. Jesus lies buried in a garden tomb. It is the sabbath day and people have stayed indoors. One man, Joseph of Arimathea, dared to go and ask Pilate if he could take Jesus' body for burial, so it is now laid in his family grave. It took courage for Joseph to go to Pilate, for he is a secret follower of Jesus even though he is also an important Jewish leader. Joseph brought a linen cloth and took Jesus' body down from the cross. He wrapped it in the cloth and put it into a tomb that had been cut into solid rock. Then he rolled a big stone against the entrance to the tomb.

Jesus' mother Mary, and his friend Mary Magdalene, were watching and saw where the body was placed. Pilate, the Roman governor, ordered that the tomb should be guarded by soldiers.

All was dark and still. The disciples were still shocked and dismayed about what had happened to their friend. Their hopes and dreams for the future had been utterly destroyed—that is, until God stepped in...

Come with me now into the light of Easter morning.

*

The resurrection garden

———————— Bible background ————————

Matthew 28:1–8; Mark 16:1–8; Luke 24:1–12;
John 20:1–18

Aim

To enable pupils to realise that the crucifixion was not the end, but led to a new beginning when Jesus came back to life again. What sort of king is Jesus? A timeless king and a victorious king.

Setting the scene

The women who followed Jesus wanted to prepare his body for burial according to their tradition, using myrrh and spices. Early on Sunday morning, the day after the sabbath, Mary Magdalene went to the tomb carrying the spices she had prepared. When she arrived, she was horrified to see that the stone had been rolled away, the soldiers had fled and the grave clothes were folded on a slab inside the empty tomb. She ran to fetch Peter and John to show them what had happened. They went home dismayed and puzzled, not knowing what to think. Mary was left alone crying outside the tomb when she had an amazing encounter—the person she thought was the gardener was actually Jesus himself!

Characters

• Storyteller

Scenery

The children come from the darkened space into the resurrection garden room. There is a painted scene of the tomb on one wall. This can be a simple piece of corrugated card supported by wooden slats with a picture of a cave-type scene. For reference, see the website www.easterjourney.org.uk. A separate stone shape should be shown, rolled to one side. If the room has also been used for Scene 3 (see pages 65–71, the story of the stone that the builders rejected) the basic scenery will already be in place, with a bush shape to conceal the empty tomb, and can now be transformed into the garden background. A piece of cream calico is folded at the base of the tomb.

Props

The main impact of the room comes from the abundance of flowers and colour in the space. If you have used the room for Scene 3, pots of flowers can be placed on very low, flat trolleys and wheeled into the room at the appropriate time. Small pots of seasonal annuals are ideal, such as primulas, together with jars of daffodils and greenery. It is often possible to get a special deal from a local greengrocer or nursery when buying in bulk. As a rough guide, approximately 100 bunches of daffodils and 30–40 individual primulas would be ample, but much depends on space and budget. The idea is to create a riot of colour and scent as the children enter the room. If the room has already been used for Scene 3, some tall plants and greenery can be left in the room all the time.

A water feature could be used to enhance the atmosphere and a hidden CD player could be playing suitable soothing music, such as 'Becoming still' by Simeon Wood (*Celtic Heart* CD from www.simeonwood.com), as the children come in.

NB: It is important to leave the flowers overnight in a cool dark place and keep them well watered if you are expecting them to last for several days. They also make excellent gifts for the team at the end of the experience.

Lighting

The lighting needed depends on the room used. It is important to create a bright and cheerful space. If the space is naturally dark, add uplighters and lamps to enhance the natural light.

Script: The resurrection garden

As the children come into the resurrection room, they should sit in groups of five or six with their leader.

Storyteller: Can you imagine it? On the Saturday of that week, everything was very quiet. It was the sabbath—a day of rest—and people stayed indoors. It was a day of great sadness for Jesus' friends. Their world had come to an end. Their leader had been killed and it seemed that nothing would be the same again. All they could do was to wait in stunned silence. It was as if the world was holding its breath.

But the women who had followed Jesus wanted to be near him one last time. They had seen where his body had been buried—in a cave in a garden. And so, very early on Sunday morning, Mary Magdalene left the house where she was staying. She carried perfume with her, which in her tradition was used to give a proper burial to those who had died.

As Mary Magdalene crept into the garden, she was worrying because she knew that a great stone had been rolled across the entrance of the cave. But when she arrived, she was surprised to see that the stone had been rolled back.

'What's happened?' Mary thought. 'Has someone taken Jesus' body away?' She rushed back to tell Peter and John. They ran ahead of her and when they came to the garden Peter even dared to go inside the cave. There were the grave clothes lying neatly folded on the stone slab, but the body wasn't there. Something strange had happened. Worried, puzzled and thinking the worst, Peter and John ran back to tell the other disciples.

Mary was left on her own outside the tomb. She was crying. The person who had changed everything for her was gone and now even his body had been taken away. Through tearstained eyes she saw a man in the garden. She thought he was the gardener and said, 'Sir, if you have taken his body away, please tell me, so I can go and get him.'

Then, quietly, simply, she heard him say her name: 'Mary'. Immediately, Mary knew that it was Jesus. 'My Lord,' she said. Jesus was alive! He had said something about this before but his friends hadn't realised what he meant. 'After three days'... 'The stone that was rejected will become the most important'… Jesus was alive in a new Easter way. Jesus told her to go and tell the others and Mary ran overjoyed at the news that Jesus was alive.

Jesus was alive! The message began to be whispered around the streets of Jerusalem, and that same message is still being passed around the streets of the whole world to this very day.

The children are led out from the final scene in groups. They enter the first area and sit on the floor with their group leaders.

*

Discussion and conclusion

Aim

To enable the children to reflect upon their experience and ask questions about what they have seen and heard.

Setting the scene

The children will have experienced the Easter story in an imaginative way. To some, the story will be familiar, to others it will be totally new, and many children will fall somewhere between these two positions. The group time is an opportunity for children to express their feelings about the things that happened to Jesus.

A basket of artefacts is provided for each group as an *aide memoire* for the scenes, but some leaders may prefer not to use them. The children are prompted to wonder why the things that happened were important. The leaders should be trained carefully to ask open questions and to encourage children to verbalise their thoughts. For this reason, it is important not to give the children more information than they have received during the course of the journey.

NB: Group time is intended for open-ended questions, not as an opportunity for the leaders to recap the whole journey. Above all, the session must not be used to proselytise. The aim of the whole journey is to encourage further thought rather than asking children what they believe. Having sown the seeds, we must trust the Holy Spirit to enable children to grow and be nurtured in the Christian faith.

Characters

- None

Costume

- None

Scenery

- None

Props

- The open-ended questions below (one per group), to help the leaders begin the discussions
- One booklet for each child if they are going to be used as a take-home gift (see below for details)
- A basket for each group, containing artefacts to remind them of the journey, such as:
  * A leaf
  * A coin
  * A stone
  * A piece of matzo
  * A small cup
  * A nail

Discussion questions

- I wonder which part of this journey you like best…
- I wonder which part of this journey is the most important part…
- I wonder which part of this journey is most about you…
- I wonder why people still remember this journey every year at Easter…
- I wonder why Christians think this journey is so important that they tell it every year in their churches…
- I wonder what this journey has got to say to us today…

Take-home gift

As previously mentioned, we searched long and hard to find a suitable booklet for the children to take home as a memento of their *Easter Journey* experience. There are many booklets produced by Christian publishers which contain the Easter message, but we were anxious to find something that did not assume a Christian faith. We also wanted something that was quirky and interesting for children. Eventually, we decided to design our own folding booklet to remind the children of the story. The booklet has been professionally drawn and printed and is colourful and easily produced. Further details of how to obtain the booklet can be found on the website www.easterjourney.org.uk. However, you may prefer to give each child a bookmark or other memento of their visit. Of course, it is not obligatory to provide a gift at all.

The conclusion

The children are led into a space in the final room and asked to sit in their groups while the discussion takes place. It is important not to rush this part: allow about eight minutes for the discussion. Afterwards, the storyteller draws the presentation to a close by asking the children all together to look at the small booklets. He or she helps the children to understand how the booklet opens and reminds them about the scenes. This part of the proceedings will need to be adapted depending on the style of booklet used. If there is no take-home gift, other visual aids can be used. For example, a cross shape can be torn from a sheet of A4 paper (see page 85 of *A-Cross the World* by Martin Payne and Betty Pedley, Barnabas, 2004).

The storyteller invites the children to remember that they have been part of a very special journey, that the story goes on and on today, and that as they leave the building they are taking the story back to school with them.

If time allows and you have provided an exhibition of crosses from around the world, the children can be given a few minutes to look at them. (See 'Additional materials' on page 34.) They are then escorted out of the hall to an area where helpers are ready with their coats and leaders bid them farewell.

If the budget allows, it is good to give each school a pack containing the gift of a resource book, such as assembly outlines or Easter activities, some publicity for forthcoming Easter events at church and follow-up material. Contact details for ministers, lay workers or children's work leaders who would be prepared to help with assemblies or RE would be valuable, if available.

Part Three

After the Easter Journey

*

Follow-up activities

Once schools have visited *The Easter Journey*, there are many ways of using the experience to reach out into the community. If the school is in agreement, invitations can be given to children to come back to an all-age worship service at church or to bring family members along to a public opening of the presentation. Follow-up for teachers can be helpful and an offer to take a school assembly is often gratefully received. Some ideas for such activities are described below. Further ideas can be found on the website, www.easterjourney.org.uk.

All-age service

If appropriate, use the presentation to invite families to an all-age service in church on the following Sunday, or at another time if more convenient. This is an ideal opportunity to encourage children to bring parents or carers along to church to experience an enjoyable time that links to the event. It may be possible to leave elements of the scenery in place so that the children are reminded about the story they heard earlier in the week. There are various resources available to help with planning an all-age service. The website www.barnabasinchurches.org.uk includes many ideas that can be tailored to individual styles and traditions. The service could be planned to include familiar items from the presentation and focus on different aspects of the Easter story. Some examples are given below.

Palm Sunday

The message of Palm Sunday can be told in many ways. It would be easy to use the warm-up and subsequent drama from *The Easter Journey* to begin the service, accompanied by appropriate hymns or songs.

The sounds of Holy Week

In order for children to understand the full significance of the Easter victory, it is important that they experience the events of Holy Week, including Good Friday. The following outline focuses on some key sounds from that momentous week.

You will need: a large candle, a candle lighter or box of matches and a candle snuffer. You will also need to collect the following items to make the sound effects:

- Two halves of a coconut for a donkey's hooves
- A collection of pieces of wood that can be thrown down noisily
- A bag of coins that can be jangled and from which some coins can be tipped out
- A tray of gravel, deep enough to allow a child to stand in and march vigorously on the spot
- A wooden platter and a spoon
- A cup and some liquid to pour into it
- Some pieces of matzo bread or cracker that will snap noisily
- A bowl of water
- A hammer and a nail
- A block of wood into which to bang the nail
- Some wooden dice
- A piece of cloth to tear
- A piece of card that can be wobbled to make the sound of thunder

Collect the items and place them on a central table. Put the candle in the middle of the table. Choose a group of volunteers (one per item listed above) and explain that, between them, they are going to provide the soundtrack for the most important week of Jesus' life. These sounds will accompany the climax of God's rescue plan, which comes to fulfilment in Holy Week. As you talk through the sound effects and practise them, you need to distribute the objects to the volunteers, making sure that items such as the hammer, nail and block of wood are given to a responsible older child or an adult. In addition to all the objects for sounds, some of the effects will need to be made with hands and voices, which will involve the rest of the congregation.

The leader provides a very simple commentary to link the sounds (see below). The sounds represent:

- Palm Sunday on the streets
- The overturning of the tables in the temple
- The Roman soldiers marching, and discussions with Judas about betrayal
- The events of the last supper
- The trials and judgment
- The crucifixion outside the walls of the city of Jerusalem

Once everyone has their sound effect ready, arrange the volunteers to be sitting in the appropriate order, as above, so that the sequence of sounds is correct. Explain that as each sound effect is mentioned, the sound needs to be made either by the appropriate volunteer or the whole congregation, so everyone needs to listen carefully and follow the leader. There should be a short pause after each sound effect.

Leader: This is the week that turns all endings into new beginnings. These are the sounds of Holy Week.

Pause and then light the candle.

Leader: The streets of Jerusalem were filled with new sounds... the clip-clop of a donkey's hooves... the cheering of the crowds... some suspicious whisperings behind hands...

Pause.

The temple in Jerusalem was filled with new sounds... the sound of pigeons cooing, sheep bleating and coins being rattled... the sound of pieces of wood dropping to the ground and then some coins falling... the gasps of breath from the onlookers...

Pause.

The Jerusalem Passover was filled with new sounds... the crunch of marching feet made by soldiers on the move... the sound of people telling others to keep quiet as secret deals were done... the sound of a money bag being placed into someone else's hands...

Pause.

A Jerusalem house in the back streets was filled with new sounds... the sound of a spoon scraping a wooden platter during a meal... the sound of wine being pouring into a cup... the sound of matzo being cracked... the sound of a door slamming shut...

Pause.

The Jerusalem courts were filled with new sounds... the sound of clenched fists thumping upon the tables... the sound of angry voices... the sound of hands being washed in water... the sound of feet dragged across gravel on a slow march to death...

Pause.

The hill outside Jerusalem was filled with new sounds... the banging of a nail into wood... the sound of dice being rolled... the sound of some cloth being torn... the sound of thunder... and of rain (the drumming of open palms on laps)...

Pause.

And then there were no more sounds from Jerusalem...

After a pause, snuff out the candle.

This is the week that turns all endings into new beginnings... but not yet. Before the sound of new beginnings that would go out into all the world, there was just silence... and the world held its breath.

Links with schools

The Easter Journey is designed to be an end in itself but could also be used as a springboard for other links with local schools. Many teachers would welcome follow-up work, offers of help with collective worship and advice on how to deliver the RE and Citizenship curriculum.

Ideally, the *Easter Journey* presentation should be held as close to Holy Week as possible. However, there may be time before the end of term to arrange a follow-up act of worship to consolidate the experience for the Year 5 children and also to show the rest of the school what Year 5 have been up to. Alternatively, a follow-up lesson with Year 5 could be considered. If it is not possible to arrange this before the Easter break, there could be opportunities to visit the school at the beginning of the summer term to build on relationships and discuss the experience.

There is a wealth of books and resources to help plan an Easter assembly. The Barnabas website, www.barnabasinschools.org.uk, has excellent ideas for the primary age group and there are several other helpful sites (see page 122 for further information). Much will depend on the time required by the school and the ages of the children. The law requires schools to hold broadly Christian daily acts of worship, in order to help children reflect on and respond to a spiritual topic. Schools are therefore usually happy to bring in visitors to help with this. It should be remembered that this is not an opportunity to proselytise, although it is acceptable to ask children to reflect on issues and invite them to join in with prayers if they wish to do so.

A suggested format for a whole-school act of worship

Introduction

In the style of a TV interview and using a hand-held imitation microphone, ask Year 5 pupils what they remember about visiting *The Easter Journey*. Allow a short time for answers and help the children to explain the experience to their fellow pupils.

Song

Ask the school to choose an appropriate and familiar Easter song.

Story: The three trees

Tell the story of the three trees, perhaps using some visual aids, such as three different-sized children to be the trees, a model of a wooden cradle, a boat and a wooden cross.

Once upon a time, three little trees stood on a hillside and dreamed of what they wanted to become when they grew up. The first little tree looked up at the stars and said, 'I want to be a treasure chest, covered with gold and filled with precious stones. I'll be the most beautiful treasure chest in the world!' The second little tree looked out at the small stream trickling by on its way to the sea. 'I want to be a mighty ship and carry powerful kings across the sea. I'll be the strongest ship in the world!' The third little tree looked thoughtful. 'I want to stay on the hillside and grow so tall that when people stop to look at me, they'll raise their eyes to heaven and think of God. I will be the tallest tree in the world!'

Years passed. The rain came, the sun shone, and the little trees grew tall. One day, three woodcutters arrived on the hillside. The first woodcutter looked at the first tree and said, 'This tree is beautiful. It is perfect for me!' With one swoop of his shining axe, he cut down the first tree. 'Now I shall be made into a beautiful treasure chest!' the first tree said. The second woodcutter looked at the second tree and said, 'This tree is strong. It is perfect for me!' With a swoop of his shining axe, he cut down the second tree. 'Now I shall be made into a strong ship for mighty kings!' the second tree said. The third tree felt her heart sink when the last woodcutter looked her way. She stood straight and tall and pointed bravely to heaven. But the woodcutter never even looked up. 'Any kind of tree will do for me,' he muttered. With a swoop of his shining axe, he cut down the third tree.

The first tree rejoiced when the woodcutter brought him to a carpenter's shop—but the carpenter made the tree into a feeding trough for the animals. The once-beautiful tree was not covered with gold or filled with treasure. He was coated with sawdust and filled with hay for hungry animals. The second tree smiled when the woodcutter took her to a shipyard, but no mighty sailing ship was made that day. Instead, the once-strong tree was hammered and sawn into a simple fishing boat. She was too small and weak to sail on the sea or even a river. Instead, she was taken to a landlocked lake. The third tree was confused when the woodcutter cut her into strong beams and left her in a timber yard. 'What happened?' the once tall tree wondered. 'All I ever wanted was to stay on the hillside and point to God…'

Many days and nights passed. The three trees nearly forgot

their dreams. But one night, a golden star poured its light over the first tree as a young woman placed her newborn baby in the feeding trough. 'I wish I could make a cradle for him,' her husband whispered. The mother squeezed his hand and smiled as the star shone its light on the smooth and sturdy wood. 'This manger is beautiful,' she said—and suddenly the first tree knew he was holding the greatest treasure in the world.

One evening, a tired traveller and his friends crowded into the old fishing boat. The traveller fell asleep as the second tree quietly sailed out into the lake. Soon a thundering and thrashing storm arose. The little tree shuddered. She knew that she did not have the strength to carry so many passengers safely through the wind and the rain. The tired man awakened. He stood up, stretched out his hand, and ordered the wind and the waves to be quiet. The storm stopped as quickly as it had begun—and suddenly the second tree knew she was carrying the king of heaven and earth.

One Friday morning, the third tree was startled when her beams were wrenched from the forgotten woodpile. She flinched as she was carried through an angry, jeering crowd. She shuddered when soldiers nailed a man's hands to her. She felt ugly and harsh and cruel. But, on Sunday morning when the sun rose and the earth trembled with joy beneath her, the third tree knew that God's love had changed everything—and every time people thought of the third tree, they would think of God. That was better than being the tallest tree in the world.

TRADITIONAL

Remind the children that Christians believe that Jesus died on the cross to make it possible for people to be friends with God. The Bible tells us that, three days after he died, Jesus came back to life in a new way. Christians believe he is with them today, even though they cannot see him.

Response and prayer

Show the children the wooden cross and tell them that it is now a very special symbol for Christians because it represents a new beginning. Because the cross is empty, it reminds people that Jesus is alive and can help others to make new beginnings in their lives. Ask the children to look at the cross and think about some things they would like to change to make a new beginning. Explain that Christians believe that Jesus can help people to make a new start.

Thank you, Jesus, for coming to earth and dying on the cross to help us make a new start. Thank you that you are alive today and know about our sadness and happiness. This Easter, help us to remember how your love can change lives and make our world a better place. Amen

If time allows, have some seeds available and ask one child from each year group to come forward to plant them. Explain that as the seeds grow, they bring new life and new beginnings from the darkness of the soil. In the same way, from the darkness of Good Friday comes the light of Easter Day.

As an alternative, if the children are familiar with *The Lion, the Witch and the Wardrobe* by C.S. Lewis, there could be scope for using part of the story, or a clip from the film, where the stone table cracks and Aslan comes back to life. This can be compared to the Easter story.

Other ideas for assembly or class workshops

The Easter Journey is best done as a whole in a suitable venue that can be easily transformed into the individual scenes. The appeal of the presentation is the experience of walking through the last days of Jesus' life and the anticipation of what is to come. This may be lost when the elements are split into their individual parts and, although many of the suggestions below could easily be adapted to the school situation, it is important to remember that the element of surprise may be lost for pupils when they reach Year 5 if they have already experienced parts of the journey in earlier years. However, if it does not prove possible to bring a school in to take part in the whole journey, an alternative could be to take parts of the journey to the school as assembly or class workshop themes. Some examples are suggested below.

Scenes 1 and 2: Palm Sunday and Jesus in the temple

These two scenes could work very well as a drama lesson or (adapted) as an assembly with a smaller school. It would be necessary to explain what happened in the later parts of Holy Week and on Easter Sunday if this was not going to be covered by the school later in the week. The children are left with the question about what kind of king Jesus is.

Scene 3: The stone that the builders rejected

This story is a difficult story for younger children to understand and would be best used as a class activity with Year 5 children or older, but it could be a useful starting point for the idea of Jesus telling stories to predict his own death if there is the possibility of a subsequent visit to the class.

Scene 4: The last supper

This scene could be used either as an assembly, with one class taking part while the school looks on, or as a class activity. The story ties in extremely well with curriculum work on Judaism (see page 117). However, it also focuses on Jesus as the servant king who washed the feet of his disciples, and this could be developed as a topic in its own right.

Scene 5: The garden of Gethsemane

The sounds of Gethsemane in this scene are probably best used in the more intimate setting of a classroom and could lose some impact without the dramatic and darkened surroundings of the whole experience. If the darkness and idea of hiding behind bushes can be recreated, then this could lead to discussion about Judas' betrayal and what subsequently happened to Jesus.

Scene 6: The crucifixion

It is possible to create an excellent stand-alone assembly for older KS2 children by using the crucifixion presentation followed by the stories of Mary and Peter. The story of what happened to Peter can stimulate discussion about loyalty, friendship and forgiveness.

Scenes 7 and 8: The day in between and the resurrection garden

The assembly on the crucifixion could be followed by a classroom adaption of the final scenes. The contrast between the darkness of the last days and the light of the resurrection could be created by using lighting, fabric, screens and flowers, which could be put in place in the classroom while the children are in the main hall for their assembly.

Classroom follow-up

Once children have experienced the *Easter Journey* presentation, teachers may welcome some follow-up activities for the classroom. These should be as varied and creative as possible. It may be helpful to give each school a follow-up resource pack to use. However, it should be remembered that, although the assembly suggestions could involve the whole school, the follow-up is more appropriate for the Year 5 children who have attended the original presentation. Some possibilities are outlined below. More detailed suggestions for lesson plans are available on the website, www.easterjourney.org.uk.

Palm Sunday and Jesus in the temple

Creative arts

There are numerous possibilities for work including drama and art (such as painting, drawing, collage, textile work and so on). Also, there are many well-known musical works involving fanfares and entrance music, such as *The Entrance of the Queen of Sheba* (G.F. Handel) and *Fanfare for the Common Man* (Aaron Copland). The children could listen to these and compose their own music in groups for Jesus' entry into Jerusalem.

Literacy

Use poetry and descriptive writing to explore Jesus' entry into Jerusalem, describing the feelings of the crowd and so on. Use vocabulary work to think about the anger of the traders. Write and perform a simple script for the events in the temple.

RE

Research how the temple in Jerusalem was built and developed. Find out about the ceremonies that took place in the temple.

PSHE and Citizenship

Think about what makes a good leader. Look at moral choices, such as the choice between making money and doing what is right. Discuss what it means to do the right thing, even if it makes us unpopular.

The stone that the builders rejected

The parable of the tenants in the vineyard (Matthew 21:33–46; Mark 12:1–2; Luke 20:9–19) could be used in a literacy lesson to explore the mounting pressure on Jesus from the religious leaders of his day and his use of stories to counteract this pressure. It could also be used to demonstrate Jesus' use of parables or stories to illustrate a point. Creative writing could result from this session, and the story can also lead to a discussion of moral choices.

The last supper

Creative arts

There are numerous paintings depicting the last supper. One of the most famous is the one by Leonardo Da Vinci. This picture could be used to explore the story through Renaissance art. Paintings from different periods and cultures can be compared.

Literacy

The story of the last supper lends itself to drama, role-play, poetry and creative writing.

RE

Most primary schools will study Judaism as part of the locally agreed syllabus. The story of the last supper is useful when discussing the Jewish festival of the Passover and the historical background of the celebration. The teaching in the story also leads to work on the sacraments in the Christian faith, especially as the Christian sacrament of Holy Communion is based on the events of the last supper.

PSHE and Citizenship

There are many elements to explore in the story. The moment when Jesus washes the feet of the disciples relates to humility and helping others. Judas' betrayal first comes to light at this point and a discussion on the theme of friendship versus wanting the perceived greater good could lead to interesting role-play.

The garden of Gethsemane

The story of Jesus praying in the garden of Gethsemane while his disciples slept provides opportunities for discussion about doing the right thing even though it is going to be very hard. The story of Jesus' arrest gives opportunity to explore the idea of being let down or betrayed by friends. As in the presentation, the story could be told simply by using sound effects and music. This treatment could also be used with other stories (for example, see 'The sounds of Holy Week' on page 105).

The crucifixion

Children may be aware of recent films showing the crucifixion in a very realistic way. Care should be taken not to frighten pupils or to glorify the cruelty of the story, but to help them realise what an unfair and difficult death Jesus suffered.

Creative arts

There are numerous paintings of the crucifixion from all artistic schools and periods. Without dwelling on those that portray great suffering, styles and interpretations could be compared. See page 124 for useful websites.

Literacy

Talk about the feelings of those who watched the crucifixion take place. Explore conflicting emotions. Use poetry and creative writing to describe this experience.

RE

Talk about the significance of the symbol of the cross for Christians. See, for example, *A-Cross the World* by Martin Payne and Betty Pedley (Barnabas, 2004), which contains a wealth of information about crosses from worldwide traditions.

PSHE and Citizenship

Explore and discuss issues such as justice, betrayal, crowd pressure and so on. Following Peter's own journey through this time makes for an interesting exploration of different emotions.

The resurrection garden

There are numerous artistic interpretations of the resurrection, which can be compared and contrasted. The idea of new beginnings, a new start and change can be explored.

The individual stories that make up *The Easter Journey* could be developed into a scheme of work based wholly on the scenes outlined above. For information about how to obtain further assistance and ideas, visit www.easterjourney.org.uk.

In-service training (INSET)

See www.barnabasinschools.org.uk for information about the provision of training for school staff on a wide range of topics, including using drama in RE, storytelling and Bible, collective worship and reflection, art and spirituality, using the Bible with children, and developing quiet spaces.

Suggested plan of rooms

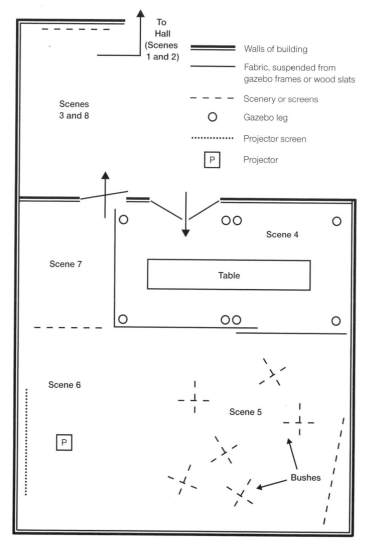

✳

Resources

www.easterjourney.org.uk
Downloads of scripts, photographs of sets and suggested plans for rooms and lighting. You will be able to find updated resources and further ideas for follow-up.

www.christmasjourney.org.uk
Information about *The Christmas Journey*, a presentation for Year 2 pupils.

www.frodshamchurchestogether.org
Ideas and information on how the churches in Frodsham work together.

www.sgmlifewords.com
www.barnabasinschools.org.uk
www.barnabasinchurches.org.uk
www.godlyplay.org
www.standards.dfes.gov.uk
www.ccpas.co.uk (child protection in churches)

Assembly materials

www.barnabasinschools.org.uk (see under 'Ideas' and 'Books and resources')

www.scriptureunion.org.uk (see under 'Your community')

www.assemblies.org.uk

www.bbc.co.uk/schools/religion/christianity/easter.shtml

Books

The Christmas Journey by Moira Curry and Gill Morgan (Barnabas, 2009)

The Life of Jesus through the Eyes of an Artist by Paul Forsey (Barnabas, 2004)

The Life of Jesus through the Eyes of an Artist (Teacher's Guide) by Jo Fageant and Paul Forsey (Barnabas, 2004)

A-cross the World by Martyn Payne and Betty Pedley (Barnabas, 2004)

The Road to Easter Day by Jan Godfrey (Barnabas, 2008)

The Story of Easter Day by Christopher Doyle (Barnabas, 2006)

Easter Cracked by various authors (Scripture Union, 2005)

Easter Days by Leena Lane (Barnabas, 2008)

Creating a Learning Church by Margaret Cooling (Barnabas, 2005)

Gazebos

Discount department stores, such as T J Hughes
DIY stores, such as B&Q or Homebase

(We recommend you do not buy gazebos online as you will need to check the quality.)

Lighting and other props

www.ikea.com
www.diy.com
www.homebase.com

Crosses from around the world

High Street fair trade shops such as:

And Albert (www.tradingroots.co.uk)
Oxfam (www.oxfam.org.uk)
Tearcraft (www.tearcraft.org)
Traidcraft (www.traidcraft.co.uk)

Seder plate

www.starbeck.com/judaism.htm (Starbeck educational resources)

www.articlesoffaith.co.uk/judaism.html (A tried and tested supplier of artefacts for delivering RE in schools)

Battery-operated tealights

Battery-operated tealights are available from many suppliers, including Lakeland (www.lakeland.co.uk), Costco, Au Naturale and other household stores. It is worth stocking up at Christmas as these items tend to be stocked seasonally. They can also be bought online: use Google to search for suppliers.

Artwork

www.nationalgallery.org.uk (Search this website for paintings of the events of Holy Week and the crucifixion)

www.stapleford-centre.org (Suppliers of books, DVDs and resources for teaching Christianity through art)

★ ★ ★ Also from Barnabas ★ ★ ★

The Christmas Journey

An imaginative presentation for churches to use
with primary schools

Moira Curry and Gill Morgan

The Christmas Journey provides an exciting opportunity for church-based children's teams to perform a delightful, easy-to-do presentation to their local primary schools. Aimed at Year 2 children, the material gives pupils and teachers alike an enjoyable learning experience by unfolding the Christmas story through creative storytelling, simple drama, fun-filled puppetry and thought-provoking artefacts.

The book accompanies the website www.christmasjourney.org.uk. The material includes valuable information for preparing the church and school communities for the event, ideas for team-building, helpful hints concerning practical considerations, clear instructions for setting up and presenting the six story-based scenes, suggestions for follow-up assemblies and ideas for the classroom.

ISBN 978 1 84101 621 4   £7.99
Available from your local Christian bookshop or, in case of difficulty, direct from BRF using the order form opposite.

ORDERFORM

REF	TITLE	PRICE	QTY	TOTAL
621 4	The Christmas Journey	£7.99		

POSTAGE AND PACKING CHARGES				
Order value	UK	Europe	Surface	Air Mail
£7.00 & under	£1.25	£3.00	£3.50	£5.50
£7.10–£30.00	£2.25	£5.50	£6.50	£10.00
Over £30.00	FREE	prices on request		

Postage and packing	
Donation	
TOTAL	

Name _____ Account Number _____

Address _____

_____ Postcode _____

Telephone Number_____

Email _____

Payment by: ❏ Cheque ❏ Mastercard ❏ Visa ❏ Postal Order ❏ Maestro

Card no [ ][ ][ ][ ] [ ][ ][ ][ ] [ ][ ][ ][ ] [ ][ ][ ][ ] [ ][ ][ ]

Valid from [ ][ ][ ][ ]   Expires [ ][ ][ ][ ]   Issue no. [ ][ ][ ]

Security code* [ ][ ][ ]   *Last 3 digits on the reverse of the card.
ESSENTIAL IN ORDER TO PROCESS YOUR ORDER   Shaded boxes for Maestro use only

Signature _____ Date _____

All orders must be accompanied by the appropriate payment.

Please send your completed order form to:
BRF, 15 The Chambers, Vineyard, Abingdon OX14 3FE
Tel. 01865 319700 / Fax. 01865 319701 Email: enquiries@brf.org.uk

❏ Please send me further information about BRF publications.

Available from your local Christian bookshop.   BRF is a Registered Charity

Resourcing people to work with 3–11s

in churches and schools

- Articles, features, ideas
- Training and events
- Books and resources
- www.barnabasinchurches.org.uk

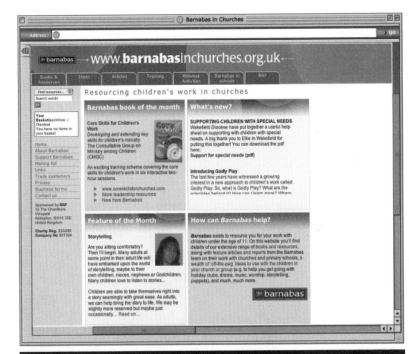